# HIDDEN MICKEYS

A Field Guide to

## Walt Disney World®'s

**Best Kept Secrets**

**5th edition**

**Steven M. Barrett**

# HIDDEN MICKEYS

A Field Guide to Walt Disney World®'s
Best Kept Secrets
5th edition

Published by
The Intrepid Traveler
P.O. Box 531
Branford, CT 06405
http://www.intrepidtraveler.com

Copyright ©2011 by Steven M. Barrett
Fifth Edition
Printed in Canada
Cover design by Foster & Foster
Interior Design by Starving Artist Design Studio
Maps designed by Evora Taylor
Library of Congress Control Number: 2011930042
ISBN-13: 978-1-887140-92-8

10  9  8  7  6  5  4  3  2  1

# Trademarks, Etc. • • • • • • • • • • • • •

Photo by Vickie Barrett

# About the Author••••••••••••

Author Steven M. Barrett paid his first visit to Disney World in the late 1980's, after attending a conference in Orlando. He immediately fell under its spell, visiting it twice yearly with family and friends for the next several years, offering touring advice to the less initiated, and reading almost everything written about the WDW theme parks. When a job in his field opened up not far from WDW in 1998, Barrett, a Texas native, Air Force veteran, and former University of Oklahoma professor, relocated to the Orlando area from Houston, Texas. He began visiting the WDW parks every chance he got to enjoy the attractions, sample the restaurants, escort visiting friends and relatives, and find Hidden Mickeys! His interest in Hidden Mickeys led him to take pen in hand. The result is this book of Hidden Mickey scavenger hunts arranged to help you spend the least possible time waiting in line as you hunt for the elusive Mouse.

# Dedication • • • • • • • • • • • • • • • • • •

I dedicate this book to my wife Vickie and our son Steven, who willingly accompanied me on countless research visits to Disney World and added invaluable insight to this book. Furthermore, updating this book would not be possible without the many wonderful Hidden Mickey fans I've met through my website and in the Disney parks. Thanks to you all.

True to their name, Hidden Mickeys are elusive. New ones appear from time to time and some old ones disappear (see page 23). When that happens — and it will — Steve will let you know on his web site:

www.HiddenMickeysGuide.com

So if you can't find a Mickey — or if you're looking for just a few more — be sure to check it out.

# Table of Contents ● ● ● ● ● ● ● ● ● ● ● ● ●

## Maps

Tip: To find a specific attraction, restaurant, shop, or resort, turn to the Index, page 259.

# Acknowledgements • • • • • • • • • • • •

No Hidden Mickey hunter works alone. While I've discovered many of the Hidden Mickeys in this book on my own — and personally verified every single one of them — finding Hidden Mickeys is an ongoing group effort. I am indebted to the following dedicated Hidden Mickey lovers for alerting me to a number of Hidden Mickeys I might otherwise have missed. Thanks to each and every one of you for putting me on the track of one or more of these WDW treasures and, in some cases, also helping me verify them. Extra special thanks to Sharon Dale for spotting over 200 Hidden Mickeys and to Jesse Kline for finding over 100 of these elusive gems!

Names in bold have spotted 10 or more. You can find each person's contribution(s) by visiting my website, www.HiddenMickeysGuide.com.

Candi A., Maxine A., Nancy A., Frank Abbamonte, Scott Abney, Alex Abrahamzon, Debbie Acres, Jonah Adams, Kaitlyn Rae Adams, Ron Adams, Sarah Adams, Nancy Ahlsen, Michael Akers, Lindsey Albrecht, James Algatt, Matt Allgaier, Anthony Almeyda, Jordan Altug, Eric and Danielle Ambielli, Cathy Ames, John Ames, Amy Amyot, Chelsea Anderson, Michelle Anderson, Robert Anderson, Sarah Anzjon, Kristin Archibald, Elena Argaluza, Jennifer Ashley, Mark and Dean Ashwaite, Michelle Astuti, Tacey Atkinson, Barb B., Dan B., Devon B., Jason B., Jessica B., Andrew Babb, Sarah Bagwell, Tony and Matthew and Caroline and Stephanie Banzer, Salina Barbosa, Daniel Barrach, Steven Madison Barrett, Vickie Barrett, Chris Barry, Diana Barry, Diane Barry, Samantha Barry, Nicholas Bartoli, Johnny Bartolomeo, **James Baublitz**, Sarah Baywell, Penny and Jeff Beam, Brittany and Craig Bedelyon, Jonathan Beer, Leila Beikmohamadi, **Annmarie and David and Josh and Rick Benavidez**, Rich Benneau, Richard Bent, Clark Benton, Jeffrey Berg, Patti Berg, Bryan and Stacy and Jenna Berger, David Berry, **David and Celia Berset**, Jenny Bess, Tom Binder, Andy Birkett, Murray Bishop, Roberta Blackburn, Mark Blackie, **Erin Blackwell**, Trevor Blair, Louis Blanco, **Nancy Blevins**, Laurie and Rebecca Bloodworth, The Bodmann Family,

Jennifer Bogdan, Rich Bonneau, Michael Bonnett, Jr., Kevin Booton, Storie Borgman, Katie Borland, Craig Boudreaux, Alicia Bourne, Wendy Bowen, The Bowles Family, Holly Bowling, Donna Brackin, Alan Brainard, Brent Brandon, Tina Brannen, Todd Breakey, Matthew Brennan, J. Bridge, Christine Bristow, Colin Brooks, Daniel Brookwell, Stephen Brookwell, Jaye Brown, Jeff Brown, Karen Brown and daughter, Peter Brown, Roberta Brown, The Brown Family, John and Susan P. Bruederle, Paul Brune and family, Erica Bryant, The Buaas Family, Cheryl Buchanan, Earl Burbridge, Nancy Burke, Lisa Burleson, Jon Bushee, Brett Butcher, Ruth Butler and daughter, Giovanni C., Villa Cadlle, Bret Caldwell, **Peter Caldwell**, Kerri Callahan, Sarah Callanan, Anne Campbell, Lisa Campbell, Rob and Annabel Campbell, Craig Canady, Jason Cannons, Stan Carder, Chris Carlson, Gary Carr, Kacey Cassette, Robbie Castro, Alexis Cavileer, Mary Anne Ceci, Christina Cella, Kelly Challand, Austin Chanu, J. Chappa, Julie Chappa, Catherine Chiarello, Dana Christos, Alyssa Ciaccio, Vito Ciaccio, Michael Ciampi, Anne-Marie L. Clanton and family, Matt Clarke, Matthew Clemons, Malcolm Cleveland, John Clover, Alexa Cohen, Serena Anne Cohen, Rob Coile and daughter, Elizabeth Coler, John Coliton, Kent Collins, Mary Jo Collins, Michael Collins, Jason Colpitts, Eleanor Coltman, Greg Conlin, Joey Connors, Jeffrey Contompasis, Lindsay Contreras, Timmy Coogan, Ian Cordle, Colleen Costello, Calvin Cotanche, Bill Cote, Angela Coutavas, Sara Cox, Karen Crabtree, David Craig, George Crippen, Rob Croskery, Lydia and Michael Cross, Kasie Culp, Erica Culver, Nancy Curl, Brian Currier, Traci Curth, Curtis D., Katie D., Nick D., Marie and Bruce Daigneault, **Sharon and Chloe Dale**, Christina Darce and brother, Jim Darling, Christopher Dash, Bob Decker, Keenan DeFrisco, Amy Degenstein, Dwayne Degler, Bethany and Christine DeLaurentis, Robert Delgado, Mike Demopoulos, Michael DeRose, Stephen DeSanto, Rich DeTeresa, **Tim Devine**, Dania Dewese, Sondra Dewey, James Dezern, The DiBenedetto Family, Cara Di Cicco, The Digon Family, Doug Dillard, James and Jennifer DiMaggio, Suzannah DiMarzio, Max Dinan, Sam Dinan, Mark Dingman, Mario DiPlacido, Calvin Dolsay, Gina Dorkins, Laura Dubberly, James Duggan, Joey Duggan, Tom Durr, Abby Dwyer, Alex Dwyer, Ian Dwyer,

9

John Early, Jason Ebels, Susan Edgington, Erik Edstrom, Seth Edward, Nicholas Elardo, M. Eldred, Amber Ellis, Eric England, Lillie England, Kelly and Kimberly Erickson, Nick Exley, Eric Fabian, Nick Falco, Adam Fanjoy, Ken Fanti, Ronald and Gianna Fazio, Joshua and Krystina Fears, Alan and Craig Fergus, Ronald Ferraco, Kathy Fetters, Dom Fiandra, Elaine Finnigan, Ashley Rae Fischer, Dennis Flath, Sharon Flood, Jessica Flowers, Dave Flynn, Stephanie Foley, Melissa and Jacob Forbes, Chet Ford, Joseph Fortenbaugh, Joe Franceschino, Sr. and Joe Franceschino, Jessica and Brent Fraser, Debbie Frazier, Eden Frazier, Matt Freeman, Connie Freese, T.J. Frey, Devon Friedman, Rachel Friedman, Ryan and Fairen Frisinger, Jake Fruci, Diane Furtado, Eric Gagnon, Michelle Gala, **Jason Gall**, Justine Gamale, Brad Garfinkel, Marilyn Garfinkel, Scott Garland, Tony Garon, Kristen Gartrell, Terry and Julia Garvey, Christy Gattis, Pauline Gibson, Kaela and Ryan and Jake Gilbert, Chase Goeser, Mark Goldhaber, Nathan Goley, Jeremiah Good, Ty Goode, Andrew Goodwill, June Goodwill, William Goodwill, Trevor Goren, James and Edward Goring, Ryan Goukler, Josh Graham, Jeff and Joyce Grant, Tim Grassey, Dani Gray, Jim Greenhouse, Mark Greenwald, Rick Gregg, Bill Griffin, Robert Grohman, Louis Guidry, Amanda Gunn, Elizabeth Gutman, Ryan Gutzat, Chris and Cindy H., Christine H., Cindy H., Rick Haas, Brandi Hall, Byron Hall, Melanie Hall, Mike Hamilton, Shannon Hamilton, Theresa Hamway, Jake Hardin, Donna Hardter, Ray Harkness, Ed Harriger, Brian Harshberger, Grant Hart and brother, David Hartzell, Bernice Hasher, Laura and Ross Haston, Bryan Hauser, Abbi Hawthorne, Debbie Hayden, Colin Healy, Sean Heard, Ryan Hecht, Mary Heidenberg, Kurt Heinecke, Haley Heintz, Claudia and Ralph Hemsley, Brian Henry, Otto Hernandez, Louise Herrick, Ricky Hett, Jamie Lee Hindes, Jim Hines, Joan Hinkle, Matt Hochberg, Rick Hoefinghoff, Ed Hoffman, Paul Hoffman, sdmt Hogan, Chip Holland, Vivian Holland, Michael Hollingsworth, Joyce Holroyd, Jamie Holz, Craig Hood, Evelyn Horton, Kim Howe, Erik Hubbard, Emily and Lynette Huey, Elton Hughes, Brennan Huizinga, William Huntley, Cameron Hutt, The Huwar and Fabanich Family, **Bill and Donna Iadonisi**, Dawn and Megan Ilsley, The Ilsley Family, Alex Inman, Andy Inserra, Mike Ireland, Ashley Izzo,

Andy Jackson, Mark Jackson, Andy Jasinski, Mark Jeffries, Chris Johnson, Jessica Johnson, Trisha Johnson, Samantha and John and Brian Jonckheere, Laura Jones, The Jones Family, Tim Jones, Michelle June, Michael Kania, Gary Kaplow, Debbie Karnes, Ray Kastner, Constance Katsafanas, Brent William Kee, Aaron and Evan Keller, Gayle Keller, Jennifer Keller, Robert Keller, Jim Kelly, Melanie Kemper, The Kemper Family, Deb Kendall, Jasmine Kennedy, John Kessel, Brian Keys, Sam Kimport, Bonnie King, James King, Chris Kirchein, Rachel Kirk, Maggie Kirkwood, Rochelle Klay, Aaron Klein, Cheryl Klein, Patty Klein, Patty and Patrick and Adam and Megan Klein, Paul and Michelle Klein, Mitchell Michini Klepac, **Jesse and Jordan Kline**, Jordan Kline, Sarah Kline, John Koerber, Deb Koma, Gloria Konsler, Rich Kordalski, Jack Koss, Jack and John and Christine Koss, Wendy Kraemer, Monte Kremin, Tim Kress, Chris Kretzman, Austin Kruckmeyer, Mikey Laing, Kim Lamb, Anne Langlotz, Brian Lanier, Meris Larkins, **Bev and Scott and Dick Larson**, Tim Larson, Rebecca Lawler, Daniel Lawson, Lea Ann Lavy, Dr. E. Kye Layton, Melanie LeBlanc, Russell LeBlanc, Will LeBlanc, Joshua Lehrer, Becca Leipzig, Justin Lemonds, Lisa Leonard, Jennifer Leone, Linda Lesar, Angie Leslie, Jessica Levenson, Billy Lewis, Bradley Lewis, Luke Licygiewicz, Taricia Lightfoot, Kyle Lighting, Beth Lindemann, Chuck Lionberger, Sara Lodgen, C. Loesch, Christie Long, **Marc and Josiah Lorenzo**,   Stephen Lovelette, John Lovett, Kent and Pam Low, Ashley Lowe, Nick Lowman, Jennifer Lynch, Jim Lyon, Will Lyon, Linda Mac, Chris Macri, Cholle Madere, Dusty Madere, Hope Madere, Karen Madere, Mason Madere, Shane Madere, Beci Mahnken, John Majcherek, Austin Malone, Katherine Manetta, Sharla Manglass, Brent Manley, Kristy Mantarro, Frank Marando, Vanessa Marquez, John and Stephanie Marshall, Drake Martin, Jeffrey Martin, Breanne Martine, Brian Martsolf, Jake Massoni, James Massoni, Brooke Matinides, Pam May, Allison and Andy Mayo, Greg Mazzella, Kelly McAdams, Mark McCurry, Chris McDaniel, Mark McDonald, Chris McDonnell, Jessica McGilvary, Saffron McGregor, Billy and Zoe McInerney, Andrea McKenna, **Donna McMurrey**, Allissa McNair, Michala McNair, JerriAnne and Susan McPherson, Jill Meadows, Joseph Mehr, Matt Mellarkey, Amy Mentz, Brian Mentz,

**HIDDEN MICKEYS**

Tammy Metz, Sharon Meyer, Kim Michaux, H. Mildonian, Geoff Miller, Herb Miller, Rich Miller, Todd and Jennifer and Sean Miller, Stephen and Brianna Millevoi, Patti Minden, Sandy Modesitt, Aruna Mohan, Perry Molinoff, Kelly Monaghan, Lou Mongello, Michele Moody, Jennifer Moon, Sharon Moore, Mickey Morgan, The Moriarty Family, Rick Morin, Patti Lel Morris, Joseph Moschinger, Phil Motto, Scott Mueller, The Muklewicz Family, Ed Muller, Brodie Mumphrey, Baseer Muqri, Lori Murch, Marty Murray and son, Brenda N., L. Naizer, Lindsey Naizer, Kurt Nank, Michael Nemeroff, Brayson Nesbitt, Mandy Newby, Jeff Newcomb, Mary Newell, Victoria Newhuis, Benjamin and Aden Newman, Devon Newport, Debbie Newton, Darrin Nilsson, Joe Nixon, Ashley Nolf, Annette Nuenke, Cheryl Nutter, Andrew and Matthew Nypower, Denise O., Erin O'Brien, George O'Brien, Eileen Knight Ogle, Steve Okeefe, Jeff Oldham, David Oliver, Mitch Oliver, Giovanni Oliveras, Beth Olliges, Bob Ondercik, Bobby Ondercik, Rita Ondercik, Sheri Ondercik, Susie Ondercik, A. O'Neill, Jim Opaleski, Lisa O'Reilly, Justin Orilio, Orlando Attractions Magazine, Katie Ortynsky, Greg Ostravich, The Outra Family, Denise Owen, Annette Owens, Charles Owens, Curtis P., Dom P., Kristin P., Melissa P., Glenn and Vickie Pacheco, Bill Padonisi, Doreen Pakidis, Brad and Brittany Paliswat, Jessica Paneral, Benoit Paquin, Nancy Paris, Caleb Parry, Calley Pate, Bob and Maryellen Paton, Chad and Megan Paton Evans, Sam and Kimberly Paton Vegter, Brian Patterson, Drew Patterson, Kyla and Jen Patton, Denise Peczinka, Jonathan Peczinka, Tawny L. Peedin, Natalie Pence, Maya Perez, Octavio Perez, Suzanne Perez, Todd Perlmutter, Caleb Perry, Jenny Perry, John Perry III, John Perry IV, Sheila Peter, Kristina Peterson, Lucy Peterson, Tony and Kara Peterson, Steve Petty, Patrick Phelan, Martin Pierce, Victoria Pike, Ray Pilgrim, Brooke Pimental, Linda Pinto, Tony Pirrelli, Susan Pitts, Linda Pizzuro, Amanda Plante, Cynthia Platt and family, Krista Porter, Roberta Powers, Al Prete, Karen and Grace Price, Katherine Price, Kirby Price, Nathan Price, Walt Prindle, Hayden Pronto-Hussey, Caleb Pryor, Matt Pucci, Todd Pushman, Erica R., Tessa R., Tim Rachuba, Richard Rando, Nicholas Ranger, Carol Ray, Sharon Reedy, Stacy Reedy, Derrick Rees, Lynne Reilly, Johnny and Jyle Reis, Michael Remy, Kathy Riccardi, Chris Ricci, Nik Ricci,

12

Mikey Ricco, Richie Rich, Bob Richmond, D. Richmond, Richard Rick, Chuck and Sharon Ridgely, Brian Rigsby, Ron Riley, Antonio Riquelme, Jose Riquelme, Rob and Kathy Risavy, Bryan Rivera, Joy E. Robertson-Finley, Andy and Jay and Angel Robey, Joseph Robinson, Lawrence Robinson, Lawrence Robson, Geoff Rogos, Terry Rohrer, Robyn Romine, Emily Rose, Matt Roseboom, Trent Routien, Teresa Rovery, Timothy Rowe, Mitch Rozetar, Chris Rudolph, James Rudolph, Jim Rudolph, Annmarie Rumford, Shauna Rupert-Sessions, Ed Russell, Christine Russo, Steve Russo, Heather S., Steve S., Robin Sackevich, I and Y Sakurada, Andy Salerno, Anthony Salzano, Sheila Sanders, Tami Sanker, Christina Santoro, Hannah Savage, Andrew Savers, Dee Dee Scarborough, Jackie Scheibis, The Scheuher Family, John Schiaparelli, Josh Schickler, Ashlea Schneider, Julie Schneider, Sherrie Schoening, Hank Schultz, Spencer Schweinfurth, Bethany and Michael Scibetta, Carol Scopa, Mike Scopa, Jeri Scott, Keira Scott, Liam and Michelle Scribner-MacLean, Todd Seales, Jack Seidenberg, Steve Seifert, David and Aubree Serkoch, Debbi Sessa, Trent Sexton, Khrys Sganga, Chris Shank, Leslie Sharkey, John Sheehan, Randy Shelton, Susan Shirey, Bob Shoemaker, Bret Shortall, Andy Shull, Stephanie Shultz, Scott Siblovin, Scott Sigouin, Deb Silhan, Tyler Silhan, Stephen Simmons, Steve Simmons, James Simon, **Jimmy Sisson**, Bridget Skallet, The Skazick Family from the UK, Mike Sluss, Byon Smiddy, Laurie Smiley and grandsons, Bonnie Smith, Neil Smith, John Snider, Michele Snoddy, Benjamin Soto, Roy Souders, Zach Souders, Douglas Southworth, Kitty Spangler, Megan Spellman, Ryan Spellman, Steve Spevak, Michele Sponagle, Kailah Spratt, Megan Stallings, Michael and Emily Steele, Kevin Stein, Joshua Steiner, Sharon Stevenson, Lori Stewart, Mark Sties, Skip and Susan and Jack Stinson, Heather Stone, **Jay Stonefield**, Ben Stowell, Branson Strawderman, The Suarez Family, Jill Sullivan, Chris and Cathy Sutherland, David Sutton, Dan Swain, Jordan and Kenya Swiss, Joey Sylvester, Kathy Szczerba, Jen T, Jenni Tackett, Alex Taday, Sharon Tamplain, Joe Tanzillo, Jordan Taylor, Karen Taylor, Leanne Taylor, Len Testa, Samantha and Mikayla Tewksbury, Alayna Theunissen, Kimmie Thomas, Patsy Thomasson and family, Brian Thompson, Jake Thompson, Laura Thompson, Albert Thweatt, Erin Tickno,

Paige Tiffany, Martha Tischler, Kristy and Scott and Jim and Kim Todd, Holly Tomashek, Frank Tonra, Frank Tonra Jr., Frank Tonra III, Kevin Toomey, Whitney Townsend, Lauren and Steven Tracy, Kendra Trahan, Nathan Trent, Marcel Troost, Beverley Tuck, Brandon Tucker, Glenn Turner, Terry Ulrich, Melissa Uzzilia, Nicole V, Stephen Valente, Max-Emanuel Vingerhoets, Aninka van Staden, Frank van Wijk, Wayne and Angie Vaughn, Tairyn Velie, Jim Vignola, The Vitrano Family, Fred Vosecky, Christopher and Alisha Vozella, Deven Wagenhoffer, Maureen Wahtera, Harry Walker, Jeanne Walker, Amanda Wallace, The Walsh Family, Grace Walter, Christine Wang, Jonathan Ward, Rachel Ward, Sharon Ward, Kathy Warner, Mary Weaver, Dena Weber, Rebecca Webster, Scott Weideman, Fred Weiner, Joshua Weiss, Cheri Weitkamp, Max Weitkamp, Carrie Welf, Matt Wells, Robert Wescovich, Michelle Wesolowski, John Weyrich, Craig Wheeler, John Wheeler, Shona Whiddon, Jennah and Noah Whitcomb, Jeff Whitlock, Katarina Whitmarsh, Sharon Whitney, Patricia Whitson, Jack Widman, Andrew Wierzbicki and sister, Becky Williams, Carla Williams, Chris Williams, Jason Williams, Kevin Williams, Scott Williams, Susan Williams, Ida Williamson, Garrett Willis, Deb Wills, Amory Wilson, Debbie Wilson, Jeannette Winner, Darren Wittko, Harry Wootan, Marli Worden, Elizabeth Worth, Kassidy and Cody Wright, Lynn Yaw, Callum Young, Heather Young, Meghann Zanotta, Christianna Ziccardi, Kristine Zolciak, Catherine Zori, and Aaron, Aimee, AJ, Al, Alan, Alanna, Alex, Alexis, Alison, Allie, Allison, Alyssa, Amelia, Amy, Andy, Ann, Anonymous, Austin, Barbara, Benjamin, Beth, Bill, Blair, Brad, Brad & Courtney, Brandon, Brian, Brianne, Brooke, Bryan, Bryan@allaboutthemouse. com, Caitlin, Caitlyn, Carlos, Catherine, Cathreine, Charlene, Charles, Charlotte, Cheryl, Chloe, Christopher, Christy, Cindy, Claudia, Colin, Colin-Kevin-Connor-Jodi-Nana-Pops, Colleen, Corey and mother-in-law, Courtney, C.T., Darren, Dave, David, Debbie, Denise, Devon, Donna, Eloy, Emily, Emma, Eric, Erik, Evan, Foxx, Gage, Gen, Gilbert, Giovanni, glaslady, Graffix, Grant, Greg, Hannah, Hidden Kid, Hidden Mickster, Hoffman, Jackie, Jake, Jake of Lake Mary, Jamie, Janelle, Jason (Trendy-Magic), JB JB, Jeanette, JE.D, Jennah, Jennifer, Jeremy, Jessica, Jim, Jodi and Nana

**14**

and Pops, Joe, Jonathan, Joseph, Josh, JP and son, Julie, Jyl, Kaela, Katie, Kelly, Kelma, Ken, Kent, Keri, Kerri, Kimberly, Kimmie, Kira, Kitzzy, Kristin, Kristy, Kyle, Laura and Joe, Lauren, Laurie, Lea, Lea Ann, Lisa, Luis, Luke, Lyinel, Lynn, Makenzie, Marc, Maria, Marissa, Mason, Matthew, Maureen, Max, Megan, Melissa, Michael, Michelle, Mike, MOEMOE55, Natalie, Nick, Nickole, Nicole, Noah, Patti, Quinten, Rick, Rikki, rjf1423, Roman, Rumbanana, Sam, Samantha, Sarah, Sean, Shannon, Sharon, Sharon from Auburn, Sheri, Skiyalater, Snickers, Someone, Sonali, Stacey, Stephanie, Taricia, Taylor, Thomas, Tim, Toontownkid4, Tricia, Trina, Tyler, Vicki, Victoria, Wendy, Zach, and Zachary.

# Read This First! • • • • • • • • • • • • • • • •

My guess is that you have visited Disney World before, perhaps many times. But if I've guessed wrong, and this is your first visit, then this note is for you.

Searching for Hidden Mickeys is lots of fun. But it's not a substitute for letting the magic of Disney sweep over you as you experience Walt Disney World (WDW) for the first time. For one thing, the scavenger hunts I present in this book do not include all the attractions in WDW. That's because some of them don't have Hidden Mickeys! For another, this book doesn't cover many things the first-time visitor should know and do to make that first trip to Disney World as magical as possible.

That doesn't mean you can't search for Hidden Mickeys, too. Just follow the suggestions in Chapter One of this book for "Finding Hidden Mickeys Without Scavenger Hunting."

# CHAPTER 1

# Hidden Mickey Mania

•••••••••••••••••••••••••••••••

Have you ever marveled at a "Hidden Mickey"? People in the know often shout with glee when they recognize one. Some folks are so involved with discovering them that Hidden Mickeys can be visualized where none actually exist. These outbreaks of Hidden Mickey mania are confusing to the unenlightened. So let's get enlightened!

Here's the definition of an official Hidden Mickey: a partial or complete image of Mickey Mouse that has been hidden by Disney's Imagineers and artists in the designs of Disney attractions, hotels, restaurants, and other areas. These images are designed to blend into their surroundings. Sharp-eyed visitors have the fun of finding them.

The practice probably started as an inside joke among the Imagineers (the designers and builders of Disney attractions). According to Disney guru Jim Hill (www.JimHillMedia.com), Hidden Mickeys originated in the late 1970s or early 1980s, when Disney management wanted to restrict Disney characters like Mickey and Minnie to the Magic Kingdom. The Imagineers designing Epcot couldn't resist slipping Mickey into the new park, and thus "Hidden Mickeys" were born. Guests and "Cast Members" (Disney employees) started spotting them and the concept took on a life of its own. Today, Hidden Mickeys are anticipated in any new construction at Walt Disney World, and Hidden Mickey fans can't wait to find them.

Hidden Mickeys come in all sizes and many forms. The most common is an outline of Mickey's head formed by three intersecting circles, one for Mickey's round head and two for his round ears. Among Hidden Mickeys fans, this image is known as the "classic" Hidden Mickey, a term I will adopt in this book. Other Hidden Mickeys include a side or oblique (usually three-quarter) profile of Mickey's face and head, a side profile of his entire body, a full-length silhouette of his body seen from the front, a detailed picture of his face or body, or a three-dimensional Mickey Mouse. Sometimes just his gloves, handprints, shoes or ears appear. Even his name or initials in unusual places may qualify as a Hidden Mickey.

And it's not just Mickeys that are hidden. The term "Hidden Mickey" also applies to hidden images of other popular characters. There are Hidden Minnies, Hidden Donald Ducks, Hidden Goofys, and other Hidden Characters in Disney World, and I include many of them in this book.

The sport of finding Hidden Mickeys is catching on and adds even more interest to an already fun-filled Walt Disney World vacation. This book is your "field guide" to more than 1,000 Hidden Mickeys in WDW. To add to the fun, instead of just describing them, I've organized them into six scavenger hunts, one for each of the major theme parks, one for the Walt Disney World Resort hotels, and one for all the rest of WDW: the water parks, Downtown Disney, WDW Speedway, and beyond. The hunts are designed for maximum efficiency so that you can spend your time looking for Mickeys rather than cooling your heels in lines. Follow the Clues and you will find the best Hidden Mickeys WDW has to offer. If you have trouble spotting a particular Hidden Mickey (some are extraordinarily well camouflaged!) you can turn to the Hints at the end of each scavenger hunt for a fuller description.

## Scavenger Hunting for Hidden Mickeys

To have the most fun and find the most Mickeys, follow these tips:

★ **Arrive early** for the theme park hunts, say 30 minutes before the official opening time. Pick up a Guidemap and a Times Guide and plot your course. Then look for Hidden Mickeys in the waiting area while you wait for the rope to drop. You'll find the clues for those areas by checking the *Index to Mickey's Hiding Places* in the back of this book. Look under "Entrance areas." If you arrive later in the day, you may want to pick up a FASTPASS for the first major attraction and then skip down a few clues to beat the crowds.

### ★ "Clues" and "Hints"
Clues under each attraction will guide you to the Hidden Mickey(s). If you have trouble spotting them, you can turn to the Hints at the end of the hunt for a fuller description. The Clues and Hints are numbered consecutively, that is, Hint 1 goes with Clue 1; so it's easy to find the right Hint if you need it. In some cases (*Test Track* in Epcot is a notable example), you may have to ride the attraction more than once to find all the Hidden Mickeys.

### ★ Scoring
All Hidden Mickeys are fun to find, but all Hidden Mickeys aren't the same. Some are easier to find than others. I assign point values to Hidden Mickeys, identifying them as easy to spot (a value of 1 point) to difficult to find the first time (5 points). I also consider the complexity and uniqueness of the image: the more complex or unique the Hidden Mickey, the higher the point value. For example, the brilliantly camouflaged Mickey hiding in The Garden Grill Restaurant mural in Epcot is a five-pointer.

### ★ Playing the game
You can hunt solo or with others; competitively or just for fun. There's room to tally your score in the guide. Families with young children may want to focus on one- and two-point Mickeys that the little ones will have no trouble spotting. (Of course, little ones tend to be sharp-eyed; so they may spot familiar shapes before you do in some of the more complex patterns.) Or you may want to split your party into teams and see who can rack up the most points (in which case, you'll probably want to have a guide for each team).

Of course, you don't have to play the game at all. You can simply look for Hidden Mickeys in attractions as you come to them (see "Finding Hidden Mickeys Without Scavenger Hunting," below).

### ★ Following the clues
The hunts often call for crisscrossing the parks. This may seem illogical at first, but trust me, it will keep you ahead of the

crowds. Besides, it adds to the fun of the hunt and, if you're playing competitively, keeps everyone on their toes.

## ★ Waiting in line

Don't waste time in lines. If the wait is longer than 15 minutes, get a FASTPASS (if available and you're eligible), move on to the next attraction, and come back at your FASTPASS time. Exception: In some attractions, the Hidden Mickey(s) can only be seen from the Standby (regular) queue line, and not from the FAST-PASS line. (I've not suggested FASTPASS in the Clues section when that is the case.) The lines at these attractions should not be too long if you start your scavenger hunt when the park opens and follow the hunt clues as given. If you do encounter long lines, come back later during a parade or in the hour before the park closes. Alternatively, if you need to board an attraction with a long wait without a FASTPASS, use the Single Rider queue if available (check your Guidemap for a big "S" symbol next to the attraction).

## ★ Playing fair

Be considerate of other guests. Many Hidden Mickeys are in restaurants and shops. Ask a Cast Member's permission before searching inside sit-down restaurants, and avoid the busy mealtime hours unless you are one of the diners. Tell the Cast Members and other guests who see you looking around what you're up to, so they can share in the fun.

## *Finding Hidden Mickeys Without Scavenger Hunting*

If scavenger hunts don't appeal to you, you don't have to use them. You can find Hidden Mickeys in the specific rides and other attractions you visit by using the *Index to Mickey's Hiding Places* in the back of this book. For easy lookup, attractions in Magic Kingdom and Disney's Animal Kingdom are also listed under their appropriate "lands" (for example, Fantasyland in Magic Kingdom and Asia in Animal Kingdom). In Epcot, attractions are listed alphabetically and by pavilion. To find Hidden Mickeys in the attraction, restaurant, hotel or shop you are visiting, simply turn to the *Index*, locate the

**20**

appropriate page, and follow the Clue(s) to find the Hidden Mickey(s).

**Caution:** You won't find every WDW attraction, restaurant, hotel or shop in the Index. Only those with confirmed Hidden Mickeys are included in this guide.

## Hidden Mickeys, "Gray Zone" Mickeys, Wishful Thinking

The classic (three-circle) Mickeys are the most contro-versial, for good reason. Much debate surrounds the gathering of circular forms throughout Walt Disney World. The large classic Hidden Mickey outlined in the cement at the rear of Africa in Disney's Animal King-dom (Clue 91 in the Animal Kingdom Scavenger Hunt) is surely the work of a clever artist. However, three-circle configurations occur spontaneously in art and nature, as in collections of grapes, tomatoes, pumpkins, bubbles, oranges, cannonballs, and the like. Unlike the cement Hidden Mickey in Africa, it may be difficult to attribute a random "classic Mickey" configuration of circles to a deliberate Imagineer design.

So which groupings of three circles qualify as Hidden Mickeys as opposed to wishful thinking? Unfortunate-ly, no master list of actual or "Imagineer-approved" Hidden Mickeys exists. Purists demand that a true classic Hidden Mickey should have proper propor-tions and positioning. The round head must be larger than the ear circles (so that three equal circles in the proper alignment would not qualify as a Hidden Mickey). The head and ears must be touching and in perfect position for Mickey's head and ears.

On the other hand, Disney's recent mantra is: "If the guest thinks it's a Hidden Mickey, then by golly it is one!" Of course, I appreciate Disney's respect for their guests' opinions. However, when the subject is Hidden Mickeys, let's apply some guidelines. My own criteria are looser than the purists' but stricter than the "anything goes" Disney approach. I prefer to use a few sensible guidelines.

To be classified as a real classic Hidden

Mickey, the three circles should satisfy the following criteria:

1. Purposeful (sometimes you can sense that the circles were placed on purpose).

2. Proportionate sizes (head larger than the ears and somewhat proportionate to the ears).

3. Round or at least "roundish."

4. The ears don't touch each other, and the ears are above the head (not beside the head).

5. The head and ears touch or are close to touching.

6. The grouping of circles is exceptional or unique in appearance.

7. The circles are hidden or somewhat hidden and not obviously intended to be part of the décor.

Having spelled out some ground rules, allow me to now bend the rules in one instance. Some Hidden Mickeys are sentimental favorites with Disney fans, even though they may actually represent "wishful thinking." (My neighbor, Lew Brooks, calls them "two-beer Mickeys.") Who am I to defy tradition? For example, the nuts in the jar along the queue at *Jungle Cruise* in the Magic Kingdom are all about the same size. Nevertheless, although the image doesn't meet our classic Mickey criteria, many guests and even Cast Members call the jar nuts a Hidden Mickey. So in this case, I include the jar nuts Mickey in the Magic Kingdom Scavenger Hunt in Chapter 2, Clue 123.

## Hidden Mickeys vs. Decorative Mickeys

Some Mickeys are truly hidden, not visible to the tourist. They may be located behind the scenes, accessible only to Cast Members. You won't find them in this field guide, as I only include Hidden Mickeys that are accessible to the guest. Other Mickeys are decorative; they were placed in plain sight to enhance the décor.

For example, in a restaurant, I consider a pat of butter shaped like Mickey Mouse to be a decorative (aka décor) Mickey. Disney World is loaded with decorative Mickeys. You'll find images of Mickey Mouse on items ranging from manhole covers, to laundry room soap dispensers, to toilet paper wrappers and shower curtains in the hotels. I do not include these ubiquitous and sometimes changing images in this book unless they are unique or hard to spot.

Hidden Mickeys can change or be accidentally removed over time, by the process of nature or by the continual cleaning and refurbishing that goes on at Disney World. For example, the "Steamboat Willie" Hidden Mickey in the star map in Mickey's Star Traders shop in Tomorrowland disappeared when the shop was remodeled. Moreover, Cast Members themselves sometimes create or remove Hidden Mickeys.

## *My Selection Process*

I trust you've concluded by now that Hidden Mickey Science is an evolving specialty. Which raises the question, how did I choose the more than 1,000 Hidden Mickeys in the scavenger hunts in this guide?

I compiled my list of Hidden Mickeys from all resources to which I had access: my own sightings, friends, family, Cast Members, websites, and books. (Cast Members in each specific area usually — but not always! — know where some Hidden Mickeys are located.) Then I embarked on my own hunts, and I took along friends or family to verify my sightings. I have included only those Hidden Mickeys I could verify.

Furthermore, some Hidden Mickeys are visible only intermittently or only from certain vantage points in ride vehicles. I don't generally include these Mickeys, unless I feel that adequate descriptions will allow anyone to find them. So the scavenger hunts include only those images I believe to be recognizable as Hidden Mickeys and visible to the general touring guest. It is likely, though, that one or more of the Hidden Mickeys described in this book will disappear over time.

I'll try to let you know when I discover that a Hidden Mickey has disappeared for good by posting the information on my website:

www.HiddenMickeysGuide.com

If you find one missing before I do, please email me care of my website to let me know.

I have enjoyed finding each and every Hidden Mickey in this book. I'm certain I'll find more as time goes by, and I hope you can spot new Hidden Mickeys during your visit.

So put on some comfortable walking shoes and experience Walt Disney World like you never have before!

Happy Hunting!

*— Steve Barrett*

# Magic Kingdom Scavenger Hunt

Clue 1: As you approach the security area, look down for Mickey under your feet
3 points

(Note: Check your Times Guide for any morning, afternoon, and evening parades, all of which will generally have decorative as well as Hidden Mickeys on the floats and banners.)

Clue 2: Once you are in the park, examine the scrollwork of the roof of the Main Street Train Station.
2 points

★ While you are waiting for the park to open you may want to hunt for Hidden Mickeys on **Main Street, U.S.A.** (See clues 142 to 156).

★ Cross the park to Frontierland and get a FASTPASS to ride *Splash Mountain* later. Then ride **Big Thunder Mountain Railroad**.

Clue 3: During the first climb, search the cavern floor to the right of the coaster.
4 points

Clue 4: Look for a classic Hidden Mickey and a Hidden Winnie the Pooh on the ground to your right near the end of the ride.
4 points for both

Clue 5: Study the reddish rock along the exit walkway for a Hidden Tinker Bell.
4 points

★ Return to **Splash Mountain** at your allotted FASTPASS time. Hop aboard and keep your eyes peeled for a Hidden Mickey in the queue, six on the ride and at least three more after you exit.

Clue 6: Along the queue, look to your left

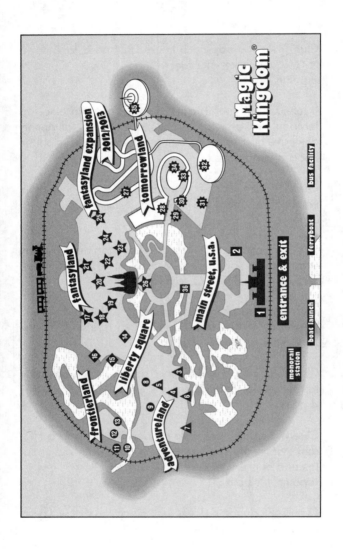

Magic Kingdom®

fantasyland expansion 2012/2013

tomorrowland

fantasyland

frontierland

liberty square

adventureland

main street, u.s.a.

entrance & exit

monorail station    boat launch    ferryboat    bus facility

**1** WDW Railroad
**2** Mickey's Meet 'N Greet in Town Square Theater

### adventureland

**3** Swiss Family Treehouse
**4** The Enchanted Tiki Room
**5** The Magic Carpets of Aladdin
**6** Jungle Cruise
**7** Pirates of the Caribbean

### frontierland

**8** Frontierland Shootin' Arcade
**9** Country Bear Jamboree
**10** Splash Mountain
**11** WDW Railroad
**12** Big Thunder Mountain Railroad
**13** Raft to Tom Sawyer Island

### liberty square

**14** The Hall of Presidents
**15** Liberty Square Riverboat
**16** The Haunted Mansion

### fantasyland

**17** "it's a small world"
**18** Peter Pan's Flight
**19** Mickey's PhilharMagic
**20** Prince Charming Regal Carrousel
**21** Dumbo the Flying Elephant
**22** Snow White's Scary Adventures (closing 2012)
**23** Fairytale Garden
**24** The Many Adventures of Winnie the Pooh
**25** Mad Tea Party
**26** Castle Forecourt Stage

### tomorrowland

**27** Tomorrowland Speedway
**28** Stitch's Great Escape!
**29** Monsters, Inc. Laugh Floor
**30** Buzz Lightyear's Space Ranger Spin
**31** Galaxy Palace Theater
**32** Walt Disney's Carousel of Progress
**33** Tomorrowland Transit Authority PeopleMover
**34** Astro Orbiter
**35** Space Mountain

### main street, u.s.a.

**36** Guest Information Board

for a red Mickey hanging on the wall.
3 points

Clue 7: Just as your boat goes outside, spot a tiny classic Mickey on a "moonshine" barrel!
5 points

Clue 8: Soon after you start, search for barrels that form a classic Mickey.
3 points

Clue 9: Just past Brer Frog, find the fishing bobbers that form a Hidden Mickey.
4 points

Clue 10: In the room with jumping water, spot the hanging rope classic Mickey.
4 points

Clue 11: As your boat ascends toward the big drop, look toward the opening for a side profile of Mickey's face.
3 points

Clue 12: In the riverboat scene after the big drop, find the Hidden Mickey in the clouds.
4 points

Clue 13: Along the exit walkway, look for the birdhouse with at least two acorn classic Mickeys.
3 points for two or more

Clue 14: Search for the Hidden Mickey in the children's play area at the exit.
3 points

Clue 15: After the ride, take another look at the mountain from the outside viewing area to spot that side profile (again).
3 points

★ Walk into Adventureland. Ride the **Pirates of the Caribbean** and find nine classic Hidden Mickeys on the ride and four Hidden Mickeys after the ride.

Clue 16. Along the left queue, spot some cannonballs.
3 points

Clue 17. Along the left entrance queue, look near a faux fireplace for a Hidden Mickey.
5 points

Clue 18. Search for two classic Mickey locks in the left queue.
4 points for spotting both

Clue 19: When Davy Jones appears on the ride, look up for a classic Mickey.
5 points

Clue 20: Try to spot the classic Mickey shadow above the drunken pirate's cat.
4 points

Clue 21: Near the end of the ride, look left at the recessed doors in the wall.
4 points

Clue 22: Don't miss the treasure room's open door.
4 points

Clue 23: Now glance at the wall behind Jack Sparrow.
4 points

Clue 24: As you exit the ride, search for some coins and jewels.
5 points for all

Clue 25: In the gift shop, spot a classic Mickey in a painting.
3 points

Clue 26: In a small camera shop near the *Pirates* ride, look around for a classic Mickey.
3 points

★ Take a short break and grab some refreshment in Frontierland or Liberty Square, which has a good fruit stand. Afterward: Stop by the **Frontierland Shootin' Arcade**.

Clue 27: Find a classic Mickey in front of the target area.
1 point

★ Then turn right to **Liberty Square** and cross the street.

Clue 28: Find the classic Mickey at the *Liberty Square Riverboat* entrance.
1 point

★ Head for **The Haunted Mansion**. Find seven classic Mickeys, two Donald Ducks, and a Mr. Toad!

Clue 29: Along the "Scenic" left-side entrance queue, search for Mickey made of barnacles.
4 points

Clue 30: In the first room inside the entrance, look for some classic Mickeys in the border design around a portrait.
3 points

Clue 31: During the ride, be alert for Donald Duck on two different chairs.
4 points each

Clue 32: Find the Mickey on the ghostly banquet table.
2 points

Clue 33: Spot plates on the floor in the attic.
4 points

Clue 34: Look closely at the "grim reaper" by the opera singing lady.
5 points

Clue 35: Along the exit hallway, stare at the ceiling for a Mickey image.
3 points

Clue 36: Outside, as you exit, look for a classic Mickey next to a gate.
3 points

Clue 37: Find Mr. Toad along the exit walkway.
3 points

★ Enter the **Columbia Harbour House restaurant** and look for a classic Hidden Mickey. (Be considerate of the diners.)

Clue 38: Check the art on the downstairs walls.
2 points

★ Now cross the bridge to Tomorrowland and go to the **Tomorrowland Speedway**.

Clue 39: Look for a shadow on the pavement near the Speedway that's shaped like a classic Mickey.
3 points

★ Enjoy an early lunch (around 11:00 a.m.) to avoid the crowds. Some suggestions: The Plaza Restaurant off Main Street for sit-down or Cosmic Ray's Starlight Café in Tomorrowland for chicken or burgers.

★ After lunch, walk over and get yourself a **FASTPASS for Buzz Lightyear's Space Ranger Spin** in Tomorrowland.

Clue 40: Spot the classic Mickey on the FASTPASS machine.
2 points

★ Go to the outside of the **Monsters, Inc. Laugh Floor**.

Clue 41: Find the moon with classic Mickey craters.
1 point

Clue 42: Spot the asteroid shaped like a classic Mickey.
1 point

★ Get in line for *Monsters, Inc. Laugh Floor.*

Clue 43: As you enter the waiting area, search for a classic Mickey in a window display.
4 points

★ Go to **Walt Disney's Carousel of Progress** (open seasonally and on busy holidays). Check the first scene for Clue 44, the third scene for Clue 45, the last scene for Clues 46 to 51, and the exit for Clue 52.

Clue 44: Admire a classic Mickey on a mirror.
3 points

Clue 45: Search for Mickey's blue hat.
4 points

Clue 46: Observe a painting on the rear wall.
4 points

Clue 47: Find a Mickey nutcracker.
2 points

Clue 48: Spot a Mickey Mouse doll.
2 points

Clue 49: Search around for green Mickey ears.
4 points

Clue 50: Look fast for a classic Mickey on a spaceship.
5 points

Clue 51: View an object with Mickey ears in the kitchen.
3 points

Clue 52: Don't miss Hidden Mickeys along the exit walkway.
2 points

★ Go to **Buzz Lightyear's Space Ranger Spin** at your allotted FASTPASS time and be on the lookout for seven Hidden Mickeys and another Hidden character.

Clue 53: Inside the building on the right wall, find the planet with a continent shaped like the side profile of Mickey Mouse.
2 points

Clue 54: Look for this same planet further along the entrance queue to the left.
2 points

Clue 55: Search for a Hidden Mickey in Sector 2 nearby.
3 points

Clue 56: During the first part of the ride, spot another side profile of Mickey. Look to the left of your vehicle in the room with batteries.
3 points

Clue 57: Catch another view of the planet with Mickey in the space video room.
3 points

Clue 58: Just past the space video room, look straight ahead to spot that Mickey planet one more time.
2 points

Clue 59: Along the exit, look for an alien pointing to a classic Mickey.
2 points

Clue 60: Spot Stitch's spaceship nearby.
3 points

★ Walk to the far side of **Astro Orbiter** and search carefully for a small classic Mickey traced in the cement nearby.

Clue 61: Check the side facing *Space Mountain*.
5 points

★ Stroll over to Town Square Theater on Main Street, U.S.A. and visit **Mickey's Meet 'N' Greet**. (Get a FASTPASS if the line is too long.)

Clue 62: Inside Mickey's greeting room, take a flash photo of the "Electricity" display and see what happens to Mickey!
4 points

Clue 63: Find a Mickey made of rings.
2 points

Clue 64: Spot another classic Mickey in Mickey's magic chest (it's sometimes covered by a scarf).
2 points

Clue 65: Don't miss Oswald the Lucky Rabbit!
5 points

Clue 66: Look around for sorcerer Mickey.
4 points

Clue 67: In the gift shop at the exit, find Mickey on a table.
2 points

Clue 68: In the gift shop, search for Mickey on a house.
3 points

★ Walk over to **The Hall of Presidents** in Liberty Square.

Clue 69: In the waiting room for the show, study the paintings for a tiny classic Mickey.
4 points

★ Now go to the **Liberty Square Riverboat** (it sometimes closes at 5:00 p.m. or at dusk). If the wait is 10 minutes or more, grab a snack from a vendor in Liberty Square or Frontierland and refresh yourself while you wait to ride the boat.

Clue 70: From the boat, look for a classic Mickey rock formation at the right end of the bridge in Frontierland. (Note: This Hidden Mickey is also visible from *Tom Sawyer Island*.)
4 points

★ From near *Big Thunder Mountain Railroad*, float on the raft over to **Tom Sawyer Island**.

Clue 71: Search one of the caves for Goofy.
3 points

Clue 72: In the same cave, spot Mickey not far from Goofy.
3 points

Clue 73: In Fort Langhorn, look around in the rear right Rifle Roost for a Mickey in wood.
4 points

★ Head for **Fantasyland**. Check out the waiting times for *The Many Adventures of Winnie the Pooh, Peter Pan's Flight,* and *Snow White's Scary Adventures* if it is still open (it will be closing for good, probably early in 2012, as part of Fantasyland's expansion). Get a FASTPASS for *Peter Pan's Flight* or *Winnie the Pooh* (if available), then ride the other two if the waits are 20 minutes or less. Search for Hidden Mickeys as you go.

If the waits are long, return to enjoy these rides during an evening parade or in the hour before park closing.

★ Try to find five Hidden Mickeys as you enjoy **Snow White's Scary Adventures**. Look for the first two in the mural in the loading area.

Clue 74: Find a red classic Mickey on the Dwarves' laundry.
3 points

Clue 75: Look for three gray stones that form another classic Mickey.
2 points

Clue 76: During the ride, look closely behind the Wicked Queen to find a classic Mickey.
1 point

Clue 77: Pay attention to the turtle shell!
3 points

Clue 78: Then keep your eyes peeled for Mickey Mouse dressed as a Dwarf.
4 points

★ Go to **Peter Pan's Flight** (or return during—or after—your FASTPASS window).

Clue 79: Study the overhead attraction sign at the entrance for two decent Mickey images.
5 points for spotting both

Clue 80: Just before you get to the entrance queue turnstile, look closely at the bark of the trees facing the loading area to find a classic Hidden Mickey.
3 points

Clue 81: As your ship takes off, stare down to your right for a Hidden Mickey on a table.
4 points

Clue 82: Keep looking down for a brown classic Mickey on the ground.
5 points

★ If you're lucky, you may spot Mickey on the rotating moon and earn yourself some bonus points.
5 bonus points

Clue 83: Search for a classic Mickey near mermaids.
3 points

★ Line up for *The Many Adventures of Winnie the Pooh* (or return during—or after—your FAST-PASS window). Study Mr. Sanders' big tree.

Clue 84: Search for a Mickey made of rocks embedded in the tree.
3 points

Clue 85: Look for a submarine image in the wood of the tree. (Tip: This is a hidden tribute rather than a Hidden Mickey.)
4 points

Clue 86: Find a side profile of Mickey in the bark.
4 points

Clue 87: Next check out a Hidden Mickey inside the entryway play area.
2 points

★ Now hop in your honey pot and find six Hidden characters.

Clue 88: Examine the flower pot marker in Rabbit's Garden.
3 points

Clue 89: In Owl's house, find the picture of Mr. Toad and Owl.
3 points

Clue 90: Near the end of Owl's house,

locate a picture of Mole with Winnie the Pooh.
3 points

★ See **Mickey's PhilharMagic** or get a FAST-PASS to enjoy it later if the wait is too long.

Clue 91: In the first waiting area inside, squint at the wall mural.
4 points for two or more

Clue 92: Inside the main theater, examine the border of the video screen.
2 points

Clue 93: Look for a shadow Mickey on a table.
4 points

Clue 94: Stare at Ariel's jewels for a classic Mickey in a ring.
5 points

Clue 95: During the show, keep alert for a classic Mickey during the magic carpet ride.
5 points

Clue 96: Stop in the gift shop at the exit and find a classic Mickey.
3 points

★ Enter The **Pinocchio Village Haus** restaurant.

Clue 97: Look for a tiny, dark classic Mickey on the wall near the exit to the restrooms.
4 points

Clue 98: Keep searching on this wall for a tiny, white classic Mickey.
5 points

★ Stroll over to **Fairytale Garden**.

Clue 99: Find a classic Mickey on a light pole.
3 points

Clue 100: Search for a Hidden Character on a wall.
4 points

★ Go to **"it's a small world"** and try to spot three classic Hidden Mickeys:

Clue 101: In the Africa room, look up at the vine with purple leaves.
3 points

Clue 102: Study the South America room for a classic Mickey on the floor.
3 points

Clue 103: In the South Pacific Room, search for an animal classic Mickey.
3 points

★ As you exit, head **toward Peter Pan's Flight**.

Clue 104: Find grapes arranged like a classic Mickey.
2 points

★ Walk over to **Sir Mickey's Store**.

Clue 105: Observe a classic Mickey outside the store.
1 point

Clue 106: Gaze inside a display window of the store to find more classic Mickeys.
4 points for two or more

★ Enter the **Castle Couture** shop.

Clue 107: Search high on a wall for a bronze frieze with a tiny classic Mickey on a bush.
5 points

★ Stop near **The Yankee Trader** shop in Liberty Square.

Clue 108: Look down at the hoofprints.
4 points

Clue 109: Look around the Square for a tiny Hidden Mickey on a shopping stand.
4 points

★ Now walk over and look inside **Ye Olde Christmas Shoppe**.

Clue 110: Spot a stack of logs with a Hidden Mickey.
2 points

★ Walk into the **Liberty Tree Tavern**.

Clue 111: Search for a classic Mickey in the waiting area.
3 points

Clue 112: Look for a classic Mickey in a painting in one of the seating areas to the left of the waiting area. (Psst! You'll have to climb some stairs.)
4 points

★ Enter the **Frontier Trading Post** store in Frontierland.

Clue 113: Look for two rope classic Mickeys.
3 points for spotting both

Clue 114: Spot a cowboy with a Hidden Mickey.
3 points

Clue 115: While in Frontierland, search for a classic Mickey in a window.
2 points

★ Check out the inside of **Pecos Bill Tall Tale Inn and Café**

Clue 116: Squint for a classic Mickey on a plate that's sitting on a ledge.
4 points

Clue 117: Look up to the lights for Mickey!
5 points

Clue 118: Outside Pecos Bill's Café, search for Simba.
4 points

★ Head for Adventureland. Pick up a FASTPASS for *Jungle Cruise*, if available. Then head on over to see **The Enchanted Tiki Room**.

Clue 119: Find classic Mickeys at the bottom of two bird perches. One is in the left corner as you enter and you'll find the other

in the right corner as you exit.
3 points each

Clue 120: Near the entrance to *The Enchanted Tiki Room*, look around for a Hidden Mickey on a statue.
3 points

Clue 121: Study the cement for a tiny classic Mickey between the Agrabah Bazaar shop and the *Magic Carpets of Aladdin* ride.
4 points

★ Eat an early dinner either before or after riding *Jungle Cruise*. One choice: The Crystal Palace buffet. Disney characters visit your table there, but reservations are usually needed unless you're both early and lucky.

★ Ride **Jungle Cruise** during your FASTPASS window and search for five Hidden Mickeys and two Hidden Donalds.

Clue 122: Study the sign outside for a Hidden Mickey.
2 points

Clue 123: Along the entrance queue, spot some nuts that resemble Mickey.
2 points

Clue 124: Study a tree across the river from the loading dock for a small white classic Mickey.
4 points

Clue 125: Watch for Donald Duck's face on a canoe.
4 points

Clue 126: Stay alert for a Hidden Mickey on an airplane.
4 points

Clue 127: Search the riverbanks for Donald Duck's face on a native.
4 points

Clue 128: Coming out of the temple, look hard at the first undecorated column on the left for a chipped area of brick that forms

part of a profile of Mickey's head and face. (This is a tough one!)
5 points

★ Walk through the **Swiss Family Treehouse**.

Clue 129: Keep alert for Mickey on the tree trunk.
5 points

Clue 130: Look around outside the attraction for Mickey on a rock.
4 points

★ Now cross the park to Tomorrowland and go to **Tomorrowland Transit Authority People-Mover**. Find a Hidden Mickey as you ride.

Clue 131: In the last part of the ride, observe the accessories of the woman getting her hair done.
3 points

★ Walk to the **Merchant of Venus** shop.

Clue 132: Find a classic Mickey on a wall mural.
2 points

Clue 133: Can you spot a Mickey hat?
2 points

★ Now scan the wall mural inside **Mickey's Star Traders** shop.

Clue 134: Look for the train on the mural.
2 points

Clue 135: Find the Hidden Stitch.
3 points

Clue 136: Spot Mickey hats on a building.
2 points

Clue 137: Look up higher at the satellite dishes.
2 points

Clue 138: Scan closely for the road formation.
3 points

Clue 139: Find three clear domes.
2 points

Clue 140: Follow the mural around to another classic Mickey on a building.
1 point

★ Walk over to the **Tomorrowland Video Arcade** at the exit of *Space Mountain*.

Clue 141: Search around inside the arcade for classic Mickeys.
2 points

★ Cross the nearest bridge to **Main Street, U.S.A.** and search for 16 classic Mickeys as you stroll toward the park entrance.

Clue 142: Look around the outside of The Crystal Palace restaurant.
3 points

Clue 143: Check out a classic Mickey image in the Main Street Bakery.
3 points

Clue 144: Inside the Emporium store, study the merchandise stands.
2 points

Clue 145: Near the Emporium store outside, search for Hidden Mickeys on a sign.
3 points for all

Clue 146: Find Mickey in stained-glass windows high on the Emporium exterior.
3 points

Clue 147: Look for a tiny Mickey on a building in an outside display window of the Emporium store.
5 points

Clue 148: Search for repeated classic Mickeys in a display window near Town Square.
2 points for all

**42**

Clue 149: Observe the overhead moving

candy bins in the Main Street Confectionery near Town Square.
3 points

★ Closely examine the Caffe Italiano coffee cart (present seasonally) near Tony's Town Square Restaurant to earn some bonus points.
2 bonus points

Clue 150: Inside Tony's Town Square Restaurant, spot Mickey on a bookshelf.
3 points

Clue 151: Study the floor inside Tony's for a classic Mickey.
5 points

Clue 152: Now look around inside the restaurant for a classic Mickey under a painting.
3 points

Clue 153: Find Hidden Mickeys on Main Street's horse-drawn trolley.
2 points

Clue 154: Stand in Town Square plaza and look for a classic Mickey on a ceiling.
2 points

Clue 155: Look around the Main Street Train Station for a Hidden Mickey on a ticket.
4 points

Clue 156: Find a Hidden Mickey on the wall inside the Main Street Train Station.
3 points

★ Ride the **WDW Railroad** around the park to search out another Hidden Mickey.

Clue 157: Try to spot the reclining Mickey in the clouds as your train chugs through *Splash Mountain*.
4 points

★ Enjoy the ***evening parade***; you'll likely find a few Hidden Mickeys (and several decorative Mickey images) on the floats.

Clue 158: If it's the *Main Street Electrical Parade,* search for a classic Mickey on the front of a vehicle.
2 points

★ You can often spot a classic Mickey in the sky during the evening **Wishes fireworks show**. If you see one, give yourself 5 bonus points!

★ Keep your eyes peeled for another Hidden Mickey or two as you end your day in the park.

Clue 159: As you leave Main Street under the train station, search for Mickey on a gate.
2 points

★ Ride the ferryboat from the Magic Kingdom to the **Transportation and Ticket Center**.

Clue 160: As you walk onto the ferry, look around for a classic Mickey.
4 points

★ If you go through the **Transportation and Ticket Center** (TTC), check out a cool Hidden Mickey and earn some bonus points.

Clue 161: Study the TTC ceiling skylights.
5 bonus points

**Total Points for Magic Kingdom =**

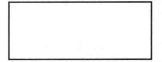

**How'd you do?**

Up to 202 (208*) points – Bronze
203 - 404 (209* – 414*) points – Silver
405 (415*) points and over – Gold
506 (519*) points - Perfect Score
*including *Snow White's Scary Adventures*

If you earned bonus points in *Peter Pan's Flight,* on Main Street, U.S.A., at the fireworks, or in the TTC, you may have done even better!

**Caution:
Don't peek at this
section unless you
really want help!**

## Magic Kingdom Entrance

Hint 1: Classic Mickeys are formed in the bell clapper designs of some of the commemorative bricks in the walkways in front of the Magic Kingdom.

## Main Street, U.S.A.

### -Train Station

Hint 2: The periphery of the Main Street Train Station roof, second level, has scrollwork that repeats a classic Mickey motif.

## Frontierland

### -Big Thunder Mountain Railroad

Hint 3: Three stalagmites in the cavern to your right at the beginning of the ride form a classic Mickey. Look down at the left side of the floor of the cavern.

Hint 4: At the end of the ride, just past the dinosaur bones on the right side of the track, you'll see sets of gear wheels lying on the ground. The first set of gears resembles a classic Hidden Mickey and the second set looks more like Winnie the Pooh. (You can also spot these gears from the FASTPASS queue).

Hint 5: On the left side as you exit the ride, a cutout in the reddish rock resembles a side profile of Tinker Bell. She's behind the fence, behind a cactus and between two metal carts. (It's the exit closest to the Standby line entrance.)

### -Splash Mountain

Hint 6: A red classic Hidden Mickey is painted on a yoke that hangs on a left wall of the entrance queue. It's in the first tunnel. Start looking for it when you reach the part of the tunnel with lights on the wall. You can spot it from both the Standby and FASTPASS queues.

Hint 7: During the first part of the ride, when your boat is outside, look to your right for a barrel with "Muskrat Moonshine" painted on the side. A classic Mickey is formed by holes in the paint, above the "s" in "Muskrat."

Hint 8: Halfway up the second crankhill, on the right side, three barrels in the lower right corner of a stack of barrels form a classic Mickey.

Hint 9: Look for a picnic basket up on a small ledge. You'll spot it just past Brer Frog, who is sitting on an alligator and fishing with his toe. Near the basket are three red and white striped fishing bobbers in the shape of a classic Hidden Mickey.

Hint 10: On the right side of your boat, in the room with jumping water, a classic rope Mickey is hanging halfway down from the ceiling. It's in the shadows behind a lantern and just past the turtle lying on a geyser.

Hint 11: The hole in the mountain at the top of the big drop is sculpted to form a side profile of Mickey's face. As you approach

the big drop in your boat, Mickey's nose juts out from the left side of the hole. (You can also see this one from the outside viewing area; see Hint 15.)

Hint 12: Near the end of the ride, the upper outline of one of the white clouds on the right side of the riverboat scene is shaped like Mickey Mouse lying on his back, with his head to the right. (This Hidden Mickey is also visible from the *Walt Disney World Railroad* train as it passes through *Splash Mountain;* see Clue and Hint 157.)

Hint 13: A birdhouse with a rope ladder in the entrance queue (also visible as you exit) has a classic Mickey acorn formation above a door and below blue roof slats. Another classic Mickey made of acorns is near the peanut shell chimney, above the curve of the red rail. You'll find it the birdhouse just past the photo viewing area.

Hint 14: Inside the huge "log" that parallels *Splash Mountain*'s exit walkway and is part of the "Laughin' Place" children's play area, an upside down classic Mickey can be found on the end of a small log that appears to be about to break through the inner wall of the huge log. Tall adults will have to bend over to walk inside the big log to see it.

Hint 15: Walk in front of *Splash Mountain* after your ride. The hole in the mountain for the big drop forms a side profile of Mickey's face. From the outside, Mickey's nose juts out from the right side of the hole.

# Adventureland

### *-Pirates of the Caribbean*

Hint 16: About halfway along the left queue, a pile of cannonballs appears on the floor to your left. A classic Mickey made of cannonballs is on the lower left area of the pile.

Hint 17: Along the left entrance queue is a room with a faux fireplace on the right side. A classic Mickey is in the plaster on the sloping area to the right and above the fireplace mantle. It's about seven feet up from the floor.

Hint 18: Tall gun cabinets stand on both sides of the left entrance queue. On two of the cabinets are classic-Mickey-shaped locks (one on each side).

Hint 19: At the beginning of the ride, Davy Jones's image is projected on a wall of mist in front of the boat. Look up at the left side of his hat (his right side, viewers' left). Below and to the left of the bottom of the "V" at the front of his hat, three tiny gold balls form a classic Mickey.

Hint 20: About halfway through the ride and past the red-haired lady, a cat behind an intoxicated pirate casts a classic Hidden Mickey moving shadow on the corner of the wall above and behind it.

Hint 21: As your boat approaches the last scene (the treasure room), a classic Mickey lock hangs on large wooden recessed doors to the left.

Hint 22: As the treasure room comes into view, a classic Mickey lock hangs at the middle of the wooden door that's swung open on the left. A long key juts out of the keyhole of the lock.

Hint 23: Classic Mickey locks hang on the cabinets behind Captain Jack Sparrow in the treasure room.

Hint 24: Just as you enter the gift shop after exiting your boat, several classic Mickeys are formed by coins and jewels in hanging plates near the right wall. Look along the edges of the plates for some of the best images.

Hint 25: After you exit the ride, turn left and find a painting at the lower right of a wall map on the rear wall of the gift shop. In the painting, a lady in a multicolored gown has a classic Mickey on her left shoulder.

Hint 26: Rocks forming a classic Mickey are in The Crow's Nest shop, inside and on

the right of the front display case. This shop is at the edge of Adventureland, near Frontierland.

# Frontierland

### -Frontierland Shootin' Arcade

Hint 27: In the front center of the target area is a group of cactus plants. One near the middle has three lobes forming a classic Hidden Mickey.

# Liberty Square

### -Stocks near the Liberty Square Riverboat entrance

Hint 28: Padlocks on the stocks near the entrance are shaped to resemble classic Hidden Mickeys (even though the "ears" are a bit small).

### -The Haunted Mansion

Hint 29: Along the "Scenic Route," a classic Mickey made of barnacles is on a huge bathtub with the words "Here Floats Captain Culpepper Clyne." The classic Mickey is tilted right and is below and between the letters "r" and "C" in the name.

Hint 30: Just inside the entrance to the first room, you'll find some small classic Mickeys in the oval border design around the portrait of the dressed-up aging man above the fireplace.

Hint 31: As you pass by the library room (at the beginning of the ride) and then the "endless hallway" on your right, check out the backs of two purple chairs for an abstract Donald Duck. Near the top of the chairs, you can see his cap, which sits above his distorted eyes, face, and bill. (Note that the chair may change locations at times.)

Hint 32: A plate and two saucers on the ghostly banquet table are arranged to form a classic Mickey. They're usually at the bottom left corner of the table.

Hint 33: In the first part of the attic area, on the floor to your left under a small table with shelves, plates form a classic Mickey.

Hint 34: To the right of the opera singing lady (her left) is a ghost resembling the grim reaper. He is holding up his left arm. Hanging from his left hand is a cloth with markings at the top that form a classic Hidden Mickey.

Hint 35: Stand slightly to the left and under the last chandelier along the exit hallway. Two lights on the left side shine on the ceiling and form the "ears" for the circular chandelier's "head."

Hint 36: Outside, at the left end of the covered walkway, a classic Mickey metal latch holds a wrought iron gate open.

Hint 37: In the pet cemetery on the left side of the outside exit walkway, a Mr. Toad tombstone stands at the rear left corner.

### -Columbia Harbour House restaurant

Hint 38: In the downstairs table area, a wall across from the food-order counters is decorated with three small circular maps covered by a single piece of glass. (The central map is labeled "Charles V.") The three circles form a classic Mickey.

## Tomorrowland

### -Near Tomorrowland Speedway

Hint 39: A tall lamp post casts a classic Mickey shadow on the pavement. It's best seen on a sunny day during the late morning or early afternoon.

### -Buzz Lightyear FASTPASS machines

Hint 40: On the right side of the display at the top of the FASTPASS machines for *Buzz Lightyear's Space Ranger Spin* is a classic Mickey with red ears.

### -Monsters, Inc. Laugh Floor

Hint 41: On the outside wall, a picture advertising a Recreational Rocket has a moon with craters shaped like an upside-down classic Mickey.

Hint 42: Also on the outside wall, a sign advertising a Space Collectibles Convention includes an asteroid shaped like a classic Mickey head.

Hint 43: As you enter the attraction, look for a window display of a city on the rear of the right-hand wall just past the entrance doors to the second room. A classic Mickey is under the apex of the triangular roof segment on the building in the front center of the window display.

### -Walt Disney's Carousel of Progress

Hint 44: In the first scene, on the right side of the stage, where the daughter is getting ready for the evening (on Valentine's Day), a classic Mickey made of cloth decorates the top of her mirror.

Hint 45: In the third scene, Mickey's Sorcerer's Hat sits at the right side of the room, next to the girl in the shaker machine.

Hint 46: In the last scene, an abstract Mickey Mouse as the Sorcerer's apprentice from the movie *Fantasia* is in a painting on the dining room wall. To spot it, look immediately to the left rear of the scene as it rotates into view. The painting is on the dining room's right rear wall.

Hint 47: On the left side of the room, a nutcracker shaped like Mickey Mouse stands on the left side of the mantelpiece.

Hint 48: Under the Christmas tree is a box with a plush Mickey Mouse.

Hint 49: On the last stage, one of the Christmas presents under the tree (near the grandfather's chair) has a large classic Mickey head cut out of green paper glued to the side of the gift. The gift is partially hidden by another present, so you see the ears and part of the top of Mickey's head. The green Mickey ears are to the right of Grandpa's lower leg and behind the present with the silver bow.

Hint 50: A classic Mickey appears (just for a few seconds) on the top of a spaceship in the middle of the television screen. Look for it just as the game starts on the TV, before Grandma starts playing.

Hint 51: A pepper grinder on the kitchen counter has Mickey ears. Look for it as you exit the room.

Hint 52: Along the exit ramps, classic Mickeys are on the backs of the round signs for the attraction.

### -Buzz Lightyear's Space Ranger Spin

Hint 53: Just inside the building, in the entrance queue, the second poster on the right wall is called "Planets of the Galactic Alliance." In Sector 1, the central continent on the planet "Pollost Prime" is shaped like a profile of Mickey Mouse's head in outline.

Hint 54: This same planet appears in the top left of a recessed wall further along the entrance queue, to the left of the large View Master.

Hint 55: Sector 2 in this same mural contains a planet made of many spheres, some of which form classic Mickeys. One of them is at the outer edge of the planet at about the "10 o'clock" location.

Hint 56: You go through three different rooms during the first part of this ride. When you enter the room with lots of batteries, look to the left of the ride vehicle. You'll see a side profile of Mickey's head in the rear left under the words, "Initiate Battery Unload."

Hint 57: As the ride vehicle moves through the space video room, planet "Pollost Prime," with continent Mickey, flies by on the right wall.

Hint 58: Just past the space video room, in the final battle scene on the ride, "Pollost Prime" shows up yet again on a wall

CHAPTER 2: MAGIC KINGDOM SCAVENGER HUNT

straight ahead and to the upper left.

Hint 59: A yellow classic Mickey is on the wall across from the video monitors that show ride photos. An alien is pointing up to it.

Hint 60: Stitch's spaceship is flying through space in a corner of the first mural on the right wall as you exit the ride.

### -Astro Orbiter

Hint 61: A small classic Mickey is traced in the cement close to a support beam near *Astro Orbiter* on the side toward *Space Mountain*, between Cool Ship and The Lunching Pad.

# Main Street, U.S.A.

### -Town Square Theater

Hint 62: When you take a flash photo of Mickey in the Electricity display, he turns into a skeleton Mickey in your photo.

Hint 63: A classic Mickey made of metal rings is in the right upper compartment of Mickey's open magic chest.

Hint 64: A classic Mickey lock is on a chain inside on the right of Mickey's magic chest (it's sometimes covered by a scarf). There are often additional Mickey-shaped locks in various locations inside the greeting room.

Hint 65: A drawing of Oswald the Lucky Rabbit is on a piece of paper at the upper right of a bulletin board at the back of the room. He's to the right of a drawing of Mickey Mouse.

Hint 66: To the right of the exit door from the greeting room, three large Mickey Mouse playing cards are held upright by a clip on the floor. In the middle of the long clip, a classic Mickey wearing a triangular "hat" resembles a sorcerer Mickey.

HINTS HINTS HINTS HINTS HINTS HINTS HINTS HINTS HINTS HINTS HINTS HINTS

Hint 67: Classic Mickey locks hang from the side of a metal display table in the gift shop.

Hint 68: A birdhouse from the now-closed Mickey's Toontown Fair sits on a tall merchandise cabinet at the left side of the shop (as you enter from Mickey's greeting area). The front door of the birdhouse is shaped like a classic Mickey.

## Liberty Square

### -The Hall of Presidents

Hint 69: On a wall painting in the waiting room for the show, a tiny classic Mickey is at the end of the object George Washington holds in his left hand.

### -Liberty Square Riverboat

Hint 70: At the right end of the bridge from Frontierland (as you face it from the boat), three rocks form a classic Mickey. They're located between the last two vertical posts that support the handrail, about one foot down from the top of the rocks. (Note: This Hidden Mickey is also visible from *Tom Sawyer Island*.)

## Frontierland

### -Tom Sawyer Island

Hint 71: Halfway through Old Scratch's Mystery Mine, bright shining gems embedded in the wall form a side profile of Goofy. He's looking to your right.

Hint 72: To the left of the Goofy gems, black stones on the ground against the far left of the rear wall form an upside-down classic Mickey.

Hint 73: In Fort Langhorn, enter the Rifle Roost at the far right corner (as you stand at the entrance to the fort). On top of the right handrail, about halfway up the steps to the top of the Rifle Roost, there is a Hidden Mickey created by: a wood knot, an additional mark, and an indentation in the wood.

# Fantasyland

### -Snow White's Scary Adventures

Hint 74: The loading area mural shows the Dwarves' laundry hanging on a line. On the left side of a pair of boxer shorts (the third pair from the right) is a red classic Mickey.

Hint 75: Below the bird and two flowers on the chimney in the loading area mural, three gray stones form a classic Mickey.

Hint 76: In the first part of the ride, the mirror that the Wicked Queen is looking into has three circles on top that form a classic Mickey.

Hint 77: Early in the ride, look for the green turtle climbing stairs to the left of your ride vehicle. The large circle on the left side of its shell forms the "head" of a classic Mickey.

Hint 78: Later in the ride, when you see the sign for the Dwarves' Mine, look closely to the right as your car curves to enter the mine. On the lower part of the right entrance panel, you'll see a drawing of Mickey (with a big nose) dressed as a Dwarf and carrying a shovel.

### -Peter Pan's Flight

Hint 79: At the lower right of the entrance sign cloud formation is an incomplete classic cloud Mickey. All you can see is the top of the head and the ears. It's just to the right of the "t" in "Peter," and Peter Pan is standing between Mickey's ears.

Hint 80: Close to the entrance turnstile, a group of trees faces the loading area. The fourth tree from the far end has a dark classic Mickey in the bark about halfway up the trunk.

Hint 81: At the beginning of the ride, as your ship flies into the children's bedroom, three cookies on a plate in the middle of a table to your right form a classic Mickey.

Hint 82: Three brown rocks in the yard in front of the doghouse form a classic Mickey. The rocks are in the brown dirt section of the yard. Mickey's smiling face may be on the "head" rock, but it's hard to spot!

Bonus Points Hint: When the rotating moon is in just the right position, you can see a dark classic Mickey on the moon, above the silhouettes of the flying Peter Pan and his entourage. Unfortunately, since the moon rotates, you can't spot this Hidden Mickey on every ride through the attraction.

Hint 83: On the rocky edge of the mermaid lagoon, three flowers on the grass form a classic Mickey; the "head" is yellow and the "ears" are light orange.

### -The Many Adventures of Winnie the Pooh

Hint 84: Inside the big tree, a classic Mickey is formed by embedded rocks above the frame of the smaller children's entrance.

Hint 85: Above the frame of the larger entrance inside the big tree is a depression in the wood shaped like a submarine: a tribute to the previous *20,000 Leagues Under the Sea* attraction at this location; thus, a hidden tribute rather than a Hidden Mickey.

Hint 86: On the outside of the big tree, in back, a side profile of Mickey is carved into the bark. It's at the upper left corner above the lower window.

Hint 87: In Rabbit's Garden along the entry area (accessed through the Standby queue), a head of lettuce and two tomatoes form a classic Mickey.

Hint 88: At the beginning of the ride, in Rabbit's Garden, the small marker with radishes (in the middle pot to the left of the "Letus" sign) has one radish shaped like a classic Hidden Mickey.

Hint 89: At the beginning of the left wall of Owl's house (the second room on the ride) is a picture of Mr.

Toad handing the deed to the house over to Owl (a tribute to the previous attraction in this building, *Mr. Toad's Wild Ride*).

Hint 90: Near the end of this room, on the right side of the floor, is a picture of Mole standing with Winnie the Pooh.

### -Mickey's PhilharMagic

Hint 91: In the first waiting area inside, the wall mural with musical instruments has several small white classic Mickeys.

Hint 92: On the right vertical border of the video screen in the main theater, a classic Mickey hides inside a French horn.

Hint 93: In the "Be Our Guest" portion of the movie, there is a point where you are watching Lumiere dancing on the table with other characters. The view goes to an overhead shot and there are shadows cast on the table from the candle hands of Lumiere. These shadows come together at times to form what appears to be a Hidden Mickey.

Hint 94: In "The Little Mermaid" segment, Ariel throws out jewels in the water in front of her. Stay focused on the right side of the screen (your right), to spot a ring as it rotates slowly from a rim position to an open circle. A dark classic Mickey image is visible just as you first spot the open center of the ring. The image disappears as the ring finishes its rotation.

Hint 95: Watch closely as Aladdin and Jasmine ride their magic carpet in the sky. Stare at the bottom left of the screen for a quick glimpse of three round buildings on the ground. They're clustered to form a classic Mickey.

Hint 96: Music stands shaped like classic Mickeys are on shelves high up above the merchandise in Fantasy Faire Shop at the exit of *Mickey's PhilharMagic*.

### -Pinocchio Village Haus restaurant

Hint 97: As you head from the dining area to the restrooms, a tiny dark classic Mickey

HINTS HINTS HINTS HINTS HINTS HINTS HINTS HINTS HINTS HINTS HINTS HINTS HINTS appears above the word "dreams" on the left wall near the exit to the restrooms.

Hint 98: On the left side of this "When You Wish Upon A Star" mural (near the exit to the restrooms), a tiny white classic Mickey is near a sparkling star. It's to the left of the Fairy, at the level of her mid right thigh, and her right thumb points to it.

### -Fairytale Garden

Hint 99: At the base of the first light pole on the right as you enter, a classic Mickey that looks like a piece of different colored stucco is in the cement on the side next to the fence.

Hint 100: A side profile of Pluto's head is on the wall, upper left of the stage. It's left of the brick circle and above the stairs.

### -"it's a small world"

Hint 101: Toward the end of the Africa room, vines on the right above the giraffes and to the left of your boat have purple leaves shaped like classic Mickey heads.

Hint 102: In the South America room, a pumpkin and two pineapples on the floor to the right of the boat form a classic Mickey.

Hint 103: Near the end of the South Pacific room, several koala bears hang on a tree. As you approach the bears on your left, the back of the blue bear's head forms a classic Mickey.

### -Near Peter Pan's Flight

Hint 104: Between *Peter Pan's Flight* and the restrooms nearby (next to Liberty Square), you'll find paintings of grape clusters on the walls. The lower three grapes in the second cluster from the right at the bottom form a classic Mickey.

### -Sir Mickey's Store

Hint 105: You'll find a classic Mickey toward the top of the store's sign-shield. The shield is hanging under a vine, across from Tinker Bell's Treasures shop.

Hint 106: In a display window to the right of the main entrance to the store, classic Mickeys are on the border of the archer's collar in a painting on the rear wall of the display. You can also usually find classic Mickeys made by arrangements of buttons on the floor of the display.

### -Castle Couture shop

Hint 107: To find a tiny classic Mickey on the wall, walk through the entrance doors to the right of the Cinderella fountain. Then turn right and look up at the bronze horizontal frieze near the ceiling. You'll spot a series of arches over bushes with flowers. Walk forward to the far end of the frieze and count back six arches to a bush with three flowers at its upper left that form a classic Mickey. If you have trouble spotting it, ask a Cast Member to point it out for you.

## Liberty Square

### -Outside The Yankee Trader shop

Hint 108: A classic Mickey with hoofprints for ears and a water utility cover for a head can be found in the cement equidistant between The Yankee Trader shop and the Columbia Harbour House restaurant, near the red cement.

Hint 109: A tiny red classic Mickey is painted on a finger on the side of Madame Leota's shopping stand.

### -Ye Olde Christmas Shoppe

Hint 110: Inside the shop, a classic Hidden Mickey is formed by three logs in the upper left corner of a stack of logs in the framed log collage under a register in the middle of the store.

### -Liberty Tree Tavern

Hint 111: Look for a spice rack to the right

of the fireplace on the rear wall of the waiting area. A small still-life painting on the spice rack contains three grapes that form a classic Mickey.

Hint 112: Turn left from the waiting area and go up the stairs. Then turn right and enter a brown room with a fireplace on the inside. Go up to the fireplace (you'll have to climb a few more steps) and look for a classic Mickey in the clouds. You'll find it on the left side of the upper part of the painting that's hanging to the left of George Washington's portrait.

# Frontierland

### -Frontier Trading Post store

Hint 113: A "How to Pin Trade" sign, behind a register inside the store to the right, sports a rope classic Mickey. Another rope classic Mickey is above the merchandise, facing the middle entrance to the store.

Hint 114: In the "How to Pin Trade" posters, a cowboy's lanyard has a black classic Mickey.

### -General Store

Hint 115: An outside display window facing the street has three wicker baskets holding merchandise that are arranged to form a classic Mickey.

### -Pecos Bill Tall Tale Inn and Café

Hint 116: Inside the café, find the plates sitting upright along a ledge near the ceiling behind the middle of the serving counter. On the third plate from the left, at the upper left of the inside circle of the plate, three red spots behind the white bird form a classic Mickey.

Hint 117: A classic Mickey is traced on the bottom pane of a hexagonal glass ceiling light above a food order booth. It's the second light from the right (as you face the serving counter).

Hint 118: On a brick wall outside of Pecos Bill's, facing the railroad, a light brown raised relief image of a baby Simba is facing left.

# Adventureland

## -The Enchanted Tiki Room

Hint 119: Upside-down classic Mickeys are camouflaged in the designs at the bottom of two bird perches. One perch is in the left corner as you enter the theater. The other is to the right of the exit door.

Hint 120: To the right of the entrance to *The Enchanted Tiki Room*, a statue with several faces has classic Mickeys formed by beads in the middle of the forehead, above the nose.

## -Near the Magic Carpets of Aladdin

Hint 121: A charm embedded in the cement between the Magic Carpets of Aladdin exit and the Agrabah Bazaar shop contains a tiny classic Mickey. It's near a shop pole that has a strip of purple paint at the top of its base.

## -Jungle Cruise

Hint 122: Check the big outside sign. On the side of the sign that faces the attraction, three barnacles under the "J" in "Jungle Cruise" form a classic Mickey.

Hint 123: Along the entrance queue, on a shelf facing the cruise boats, three walnuts in a jar resemble a classic Mickey.

Hint 124: On a tree across the river from the loading dock, there's a white classic Mickey marking on the tree bark above the hut. Follow the right leaning tree trunk high up to the Mickey marking. It's about two-thirds of the distance up the trunk, just as the trunk angles slightly more to the right.

Hint 125: Along the right side of the boat, watch for the Pygmy War Canoes sitting on a beach. The bow of the middle canoe resembles Donald Duck.

Hint 126: After the waterfall, a wrecked silver plane sits to the right of the boat. Look back to spot three circles etched in the metal at the lower right of the visible section of fuselage. The circles are all the same size, but many folks and Cast Members consider them a Hidden Mickey.

Hint 127: Along the left side of the boat, be alert for menacing natives with spears. The last isolated native of the group wears a Donald mask.

Hint 128: The first undecorated column on the left wall (the third column from the end as you come out of the temple) has a chipped area of brick on the third block from the top. The chipped area forms part of a profile view of Mickey's head and face. Don't get discouraged if you have trouble spotting it; this one is tough to find—especially the first time.

### -Swiss Family Treehouse

Hint 129: A side profile of Mickey, facing to the right, is on a section of the tree trunk that touches a wall of the treehouse. Mickey is in a clearing inside a large patch of green algae. You'll find it on the right as you descend the steps from the boys' bedroom and on the left as you walk down from the very top of the trail.

Hint 130: On the outdoor stone seating area near the *Swiss Family Treehouse,* a classic Mickey is etched in a rock. The rock rests on the seating area against a wooden pole. Mickey's head is made of circles and his ears are depressions in the rock.

# Tomorrowland

### -Tomorrowland Transit Authority PeopleMover

Hint 131: The woman getting her hair done sports a belt buckle with a classic Hidden Mickey.

### -Merchant of Venus shop

Hint 132: Face the cash registers and look at the mural on the wall behind the left side

register. In the foreground is one of Stitch's cousins holding a Mickey balloon.

Hint 133: In the same mural, another cousin of Stitch is wearing Mickey ears.

### -Mickey's Star Traders shop

Hint 134: On the wall mural, the headlights of a train form a classic Mickey.

Hint 135: Stitch races beside a train in the mural.

Hint 136: Mickey hats sit atop windows halfway up the sides of a building.

Hint 137: Satellite dishes form a classic Mickey on top of this building.

Hint 138: Across the room on another wall mural, the middle circle of freeway loops forms a classic Mickey.

Hint 139: Over one of the entrance doors, clear domes form a classic Mickey.

Hint 140: The blue glass dome covering one building is a classic Mickey with ears.

### -Tomorrowland Video Arcade

Hint 141: Inside the Tomorrowland Video Arcade, classic Mickey images repeat on the outside of the photo booths in the Portrait Studio area.

# Main Street, U.S.A.

Hint 142: On the roof of The Crystal Palace restaurant, the circles in the middle row of the tower above the main entrance resemble Mickey ears.

Hint 143: Along the left side of the Main Street Bakery entrance queue, a Mickey-shaped serving platter is partially hidden in the upper left of a display case. Other plate arrangements in the display cabinet aren't proportioned properly to be Hidden Mickeys.

Hint 144: In the Emporium store, metal poles that hold up merchandise shelves sport classic Mickey holes.

Hint 145: Outside along Main Street, just to the right of the Emporium shop and near the Athletic Club, a sign on a door has two classic Mickeys at the top and bottom along the border.

Hint 146: The cupola above the Emporium, in the middle recessed area of the store, has stained-glass windows just below the highest eaves. Each main flower circle in the windows is joined with two frosted ear panels to form classic Mickeys.

Hint 147: In the outside *Aladdin* display window of the Emporium store, you'll find a small classic Mickey window in a building wall.

Hint 148: At the Main Street Confectionery, in outside display windows facing Main Street, doilies sport classic Mickeys along their outer borders.

Hint 149: Candy bins in the Main Street Confectionery move along a track suspended from the ceiling. On the lower front and back sides of the bins are holes arranged like classic Mickeys.

Bonus Points Hint: The sign on the Caffe Italiano cart, which appears seasonally in front of Tony's Town Square Restaurant, includes a classic Mickey in its design.

Hint 150: Inside Tony's Town Square Restaurant, as you enter the main dining area from the entrance waiting area, three white flowers form a classic Mickey on a bookshelf to the upper left.

Hint 151: When you enter Tony's inside dining area, look left to the corner and find the second floor tile to the right of the corner. There's a classic Mickey impression at the center right side of this black tile. If you view the Hidden Mickey from the seating area, it will appear upside-down.

Hint 152: A classic Mickey made of bread rolls is to the right as you enter the dining area inside Tony's Town Square Restaurant.

It's sitting on an armoire under a painting from *Lady and the Tramp*.

Hint 153: Several classic Mickeys adorn the gear of the horse pulling the Main Street Trolley.

Hint 154: In Town Square plaza, walk about seven or eight steps away from the island curb towards the train station. As you approach the station, a classic Mickey is formed by circles on the train station ceiling. You might call this a "positional" classic Mickey because you have to be in just the right position to see it.

Hint 155: At the Main Street Train Station's faux ticket office upstairs, an image that looks like Mickey is on a baggage ticket next to the letter "K" inside the front window to the right. (Walk up the outside stairs to the office window, which faces Main Street.)

Hint 156: A classic Mickey-shaped lock can also be found inside the faux ticket office. Look for the lock hanging on the right wall behind the windows.

### -From the WDW Railroad

Hint 157: In the riverboat scene near the end of the *Splash Mountain* ride, the upper outline of one of the white clouds on the right is shaped like Mickey Mouse lying on his back, his head to the right.

(Note: This Hidden Mickey is also visible from the *Splash Mountain* ride; see Clue and Hint 12.)

### -Evening Parade

Hint 158: In the *Main Street Electrical Parade*, a classic Mickey is formed by circles on the front of the train Goofy is driving.

### -Train Station Exit from Main Street

Hint 159: Classic Mickeys are repeated atop a tall gate, which is usually folded inside a

65

recess beside the entrance and exit tunnel walkway under the Main Street Train Station.

## Ferryboat Landing at Magic Kingdom

Hint 160: A rope coiled into a classic Mickey can often be spotted at the Magic Kingdom loading dock for the ferry. Look next to a large post on one side as you walk onto the boat. Unfortunately, this rope image is not reliably present; ask a nearby Cast Member.

## Transportation and Ticket Center

Hint 161: An imprint of Mickey's face, full frontal image, has remained over the years. It looks as though it was made by a balloon that melted against the glass. This Hidden Mickey is in the second overhead glass bubble from the tram, in the first row of bubble skylights to the right as you walk from the trams toward the monorail entrance ramps.

# CHAPTER 3

# Epcot Scavenger Hunt

••••••••••••••••••••••••••

If you arrive early in the day, as I recommend, ask if *Soarin'*, *Test Track*, and *Mission: SPACE* — the attractions in which I start the Epcot Scavenger Hunt — are open now. If not, do the *Living with the Land* ride (Clues 95 to 103) first and come back to *Soarin'*, *Test Track*, and *Mission: SPACE*.

(Note: Many of the Hidden Mickeys in this park are in restaurants and shops. Be considerate of fellow guests and Cast Members as you search. Tell them what you're looking for, so they can share in the fun. Avoid searching restaurants at busy meal times unless you are one of the diners.)

★ Walk briskly to **Soarin'** in The Land Pavilion.

Clue 1: Along the entrance queue, five screens show changing artistic landscapes. Search for Mickey in the landscape with the purple mountain ridge in the lower background.
4 points

Clue 2: In the pre-show video, spot the Mickey ears.
2 points

Clue 3: In the pre-show video, stay alert for Hidden Character clothing logos.
4 points for spotting both

Clue 4: While soaring, look left for a Mickey balloon.
4 points

Clue 5: Then look right for a Mickey shadow.
4 points

Clue 6: Don't blink at the golf ball!
5 points

Clue 7: A huge classic Mickey in the sky

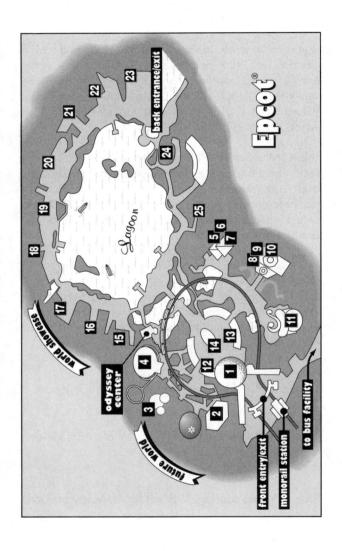

# FUTURE WORLD

1 Spaceship Earth Pavilion
2 Universe of Energy Pavilion
3 Mission: SPACE Pavilion
4 Test Track Pavilion

Imagination! Pavilion
5 Captain EO
6 Journey Into Imagination with Figment
7 ImageWorks

The Land Pavilion
8 Living with the Land
9 The Circle of Life
10 Soarin'

11 The Seas with Nemo & Friends Pavilion
Turtle Talk with Crush
12 Innoventions East
13 Innoventions West
14 Innoventions Plaza

# WORLD SHOWCASE

15 Mexico:
     Gran Fiesta Tour
16 Norway:
     Maelstrom
17 China:
     Reflections of China
18 Germany
19 Italy
20 The American Adventure:
     The American Adventure show
21 Japan
22 Morocco
23 France:
     Impressions de France
24 United Kingdom
25 Canada:
     O Canada!

69

greets you at the end of your *Soarin'* ride.
3 points

★ Go to the walkway through Innoventions East and get a FASTPASS for *Test Track*. Start your hunt in the **Mission: SPACE** waiting queue. Three Hidden Mickeys wait to be found.

Clue 8: Along the entrance queue, search for a Hidden Mickey on a planet.
4 points

Clue 9: Spot a Hidden Mickey in "status lights" on a monitor.
4 points

Clue 10: Look for waveform images on a monitor that form a Hidden Mickey.
4 points

Clue 11: Just before launch, keep your eyes open for two identical Hidden Mickeys.
4 points

Clue 12: As you land on Mars, glance around for a Hidden Mickey on a building.
4 points

Clue 13: After the ride, look for a Hidden Mickey on a video console in the exhibit area.
2 points

Clue 14: Spot a Hidden Mickey on the ceiling of the gift shop at the attraction exit.
4 points

Clue 15: Search for Donald and Pluto on the ceiling.
4 points for spotting both

Clue 16: Study the spaceship in a mural in the gift shop.
3 points

Clue 17: Now squint for a small Hidden Mickey in the same mural.
3 points

Clue 18: While you're at it, examine the

mural for an upside-down classic Mickey.
3 points

Clue 19: Now glance low for classic Mickeys near the floor.
2 points

Clue 20: Find two classic Mickeys and a side-profile Mickey on the wall of the gift shop.
2 points for spotting all three

Clue 21: Outside in the front plaza, search for a classic Mickey on the moon.
3 points

Clue 22: Look down for a classic Mickey in the blue tile area out front.
5 points

Clue 23: In a blue tile stripe out front, spot a white classic Mickey near a gray disk.
4 points

Clue 24: Find two more classic tile Mickeys near a drain cover.
4 points for spotting both

★ Go to *Test Track*.

Clue 25: Look for a Hidden Mickey among the objects on a tool chest.
3 points

Clue 26: Jut before you get to the pre-show room, inspect the "Crash Test Vehicle" in area 5b carefully.
3 points

★ Find Mickey near the knee calibration area.

Clue 27: Search out a classic Hidden Mickey.
2 points

Clue 28: If you can manage to peek inside the first (Single-Riders queue) pre-show room, glance around for an orange Hidden Mickey on the wall.
3 points

Clue 29: Now look for another classic Mickey in the same room.
3 points

Clue 30: In the third (farthest away) pre-show room for the Standby queue, spot Mickey on the wall.
3 points

★ During the **Test Track ride**, try to find nine Hidden Mickeys. (Keep your eyes peeled; four of them are hard to spot.)

Clue 31: In the "Environmental Chambers," glance back for a classic Mickey above you to the right.
5 points

Clue 32: Look for the Mickey Mouse pencil in the first "Environmental Test" office.
2 points

Clue 33: In this same office, locate a classic Mickey made by a red Magic Marker.
3 points

Clue 34: Look to the left back wall of the cold room to find a classic Mickey.
5 points

Clue 35: Spot a Mickey Mouse doll in the second "Environmental Test" office.
3 points

★ In the "Corrosion Chamber" (the second chamber in the "Environmental Test" area), look fast to the right, then to the left to spot two classic Mickeys in rust.

Clue 36: On your right, check a hanging car door.
4 points

Clue 37: On your left, look for a truck fender.
4 points

Clue 38: As you approach the crash barrier wall, try to spot the classic Mickey crash-test sticker on a white car to the left of your ride vehicle.
4 points

Clue 39: Then just before you reach the crash barrier wall, look at the floor to your left for one more.
4 points

Clue 40: After the ride, check out the monitors in the photo selection area for another look at the classic Mickey in Clue 39.
1 point

★ Now search the monitors for another classic Mickey behind the car to earn possible bonus points. (This Mickey isn't always visible.)
3 bonus points

Clue 41: Along the exit, spot Mickey on a sticker.
3 points

Clue 42: Then find Mickey on a nametag.
4 points

★ Walk across Future World to The Seas with Nemo & Friends Pavilion. Check out **Turtle Talk with Crush**.

Clue 43: Study the undersea images on the show screen for a classic Mickey.
3 points

★ Stroll to the Imagination! Pavilion. Enjoy the **Captain EO** show.

Clue 44: Check out Captain EO's ship for a Hidden Mickey.
3 points

★ When World Showcase opens, take the path to the right of Test Track, heading toward World Showcase. Stop by the **Odyssey Center building**.

Clue 45: Glance inside for Mickey.
3 points

★ Go to **Maelstrom** in the Norway Pavilion. Study the loading area mural to find two Hidden Mickeys. Then enjoy the ride and movie and find two more.

**73**

Clue 46: Find the Viking wearing Mickey ears.
3 points

Clue 47: Look for the cruise director with Mickey's face outlined in the creases of her shirt. (This is a hard one to spot.)
4 points

Clue 48: While on the ride, check out a leaf shadow Mickey on a rock archway above you.
5 points

Clue 49: During the movie after the *Maelstrom* ride, stay alert for Mickey above the trees.
4 points

★ Eat an early lunch to avoid the crowds. The San Angel Inn Restaurant is an ideal choice if you have 11:30 a.m. or so reservations. If not, try fast food at Cantina de San Angel at the Mexico Pavilion. Or try to get seated at Akershus Royal Banquet Hall in Norway (if you enjoy seafood); it sometimes has tables available.

★ If you eat in the **San Angel Inn**, look for classic Mickeys in the smoke rising from the volcano (see Clue 55).

★ Go to **Gran Fiesta Tour Starring the Three Caballeros** in the Mexico Pavilion and keep your eyes peeled for classic Mickeys.

Clue 50: At the beginning of the ride, take a close look at the smoke rising from the volcano.
4 points

Clue 51: In the first tunnel, search for Mickey on a necklace.
5 points

Clue 52: Find Mickey on a video screen on the wall.
5 points

Clue 53: Spot classic Mickeys in a small blue pond to the left of the boat.
4 points

Clue 54: Don't miss Mickey in a barge!
3 points

★ After exiting the ride, walk to the **San Angel Inn restaurant** (if you haven't already been there) and look for classic Mickeys that appear and disappear.

Clue 55: Observe the smoke rising from the volcano. Ask the attendants to let you walk to the fence by the river if you need a closer look.
4 points

★ Stroll over to **China**.

Clue 56: Search for Hidden Mickeys on posts in the courtyard.
4 points

★ Now study the water for possible bonus points.
2 bonus points

★ Cross over the bridge to the **Outpost**.

Clue 57: Check out the wooden poles.
3 points

★ Walk left to **Germany** to find four classic Hidden Mickeys.

Clue 58: As you walk into the plaza, look for the classic Mickey on a suit of armor on the building to your right.
3 points

Clue 59: Spot Mickey behind a large bell.
3 points

Clue 60: Search for Mickey near a lion.
3 points

Clue 61: Can you find a Hidden Mickey in the landscaping of the exhibit?
3 points

★ Now check out the rest of the landscaping around the train attraction to earn your-

self some possible bonus points. (Note: These Hidden Mickeys come and go.)
1 bonus point for each Hidden Mickey you spot.

★ Stop at **Italy** to inspect the shops, statues, and restaurants.

Clue 62: Classic Mickeys are near the wine!
2 points

Clue 63: Look for Mickey behind a statue.
3 points

Clue 64: Find Mickey in the waiting area of Tutto Italia Ristorante.
3 points

★ Go to **The American Adventure pavilion** and inspect the rear wall of the rotunda, upstairs and down, for classic Hidden Mickeys.

Clue 65: Study a picture in the rotunda for Hidden Mickeys on two metal beams.
3 points for spotting both

Clue 66: Take a good look at the bronze eagle reliefs.
2 points for each floor; 4 points total

★ Now watch **The American Adventure show** and keep an eye out for three hard-to-spot classic Hidden Mickeys.

Clue 67: At the beginning of the film, look at the rocks behind a kneeling female pilgrim.
4 points

Clue 68: Stay alert for a Mickey image on a stockade.
3 points

Clue 69: At the end, watch the fireworks' explosions behind the Statue of Liberty Torch.
4 points

Clue 70: Outside, enjoy the **Fife and Drum Corps** and find four Hidden Mick-

eys. Check your Times Guide for performance times.
5 points for all spotting four

★ Stroll over to **Japan**.

Clue 71: Search for a classic Mickey in the koi fish pond.
2 points

Clue 72: Check out the grates at the base of the trees in the courtyard.
2 points

Clue 73: Look around for a bamboo Mickey near Yakitori House.
3 points

Clue 74: On your way to Morocco, don't miss the rock Mickey near the Mitsukoshi store!
5 points

★ Meander to **Morocco**.

Clue 75: Gaze at the front of the shop on the promenade.
2 points

Clue 76: Now look at the roof of this shop.
4 points

Clue 77: Study a wall mural at the rear of the pavilion for three Hidden Mickeys.
5 points for spotting all three

★ Go to **France**.

Clue 78: Examine the grates at the bases of the trees in the courtyard.
2 points

Clue 79: Find the classic Mickey bush on the right side of the ornamental garden.
3 points

Clue 80: Look high for classic Mickeys on the outside of a shop.
2 points

Clue 81: Search for Remy the rat inside a shop in the France Pavilion.
4 points

Clue 82: In the movie *Impressions de France*, spot Mickey's head and ears in the background of the wedding scene.
4 points

★ Enter the **United Kingdom**.

Clue 83: Check out a classic sports Mickey from the street.
2 points

Clue 84: Look around for Mickey stickers hidden inside merchandise cabinets in a UK store.
5 points for three or more

★ Now walk over to **Canada** to find more classic Mickeys.

Clue 85: Examine the totem pole on the left near the steps into the pavilion.
3 points

Clue 86: Inside a store, search for a classic Mickey on an animal.
4 points

Clue 87: Step inside Le Cellier Steakhouse for a Mickey made of wine.
3 points

★ Stroll over to the **Disney Traders store** in Showcase Plaza.

Clue 88: Enter the store and discover a running Mickey.
2 points

★ Return to Future World and walk to Club Cool at the end of Innoventions West. Enjoy free exotic and refreshing soft drinks from foreign countries.

★ Get a FASTPASS for the *Living with the*

*Land* ride in The Land Pavilion.

★ Head over to **The Seas with Nemo & Friends Pavilion** to find eight Hidden Mickeys.

Clue 89: Keep alert on the ride for a Mickey in the rock. Look below the fifth video screen to spot it.
5 points

Clue 90: Walk upstairs and search for a Hidden Mickey on the Aquarium floor.
5 points

Clue 91: Downstairs, find two Hidden Mickeys in bubbles on the wall near the manatees.
5 points for spotting both

Clue 92: In Bruce's room downstairs, look around for classic Mickeys in two different windows.
4 points for spotting both

Clue 93: In the waiting area for **Turtle Talk with Crush**, spot a tiny Mickey in the coral on the wall.
5 points

Clue 94: Search for Mickey near the exit gift shop.
3 points

★ Head right to the **Living with the Land ride** at your FASTPASS time. Study the wall murals to find three classic Hidden Mickeys.

Clue 95: Take a good look at the bubbles in the mural at the rear of the entrance queue.
3 points

Clue 96: Examine the mural behind the loading area near the farmer's hat.
3 points

Clue 97: Now check the lower part of the mural behind the loading area.
3 points

Clue 98: Keep alert for a Cast Member with a Hidden Mickey on a video screen.
4 points

Clue 99: Search for a garden hose classic Mickey. (This Hidden Mickey is also visible on the "Behind the Seeds" tour.)
4 points

Clue 100: Spot Mickey near the shrimp.
4 points

Clue 101: Look for plants arranged as Hidden Mickeys. (These Hidden Mickeys may disappear at times.)
4 points

Clue 102: Toward the end of the ride, find the green Hidden Mickey in the round test tube holder in a lab room.
3 points

Clue 103: Spot Mickey's name in this same lab room.
2 points

★ Go inside **The Garden Grill Restaurant** upstairs and take a good look at the back wall.

Clue 104: Find and then marvel at the green face of Mickey Mouse on the left side of the large wall mural of vegetation. He's in three-quarter profile on the right side of a single fern and he's well camouflaged by the fern's leaves.
5 points

Clue 105: Observe Hidden Mickeys on the characters' clothing.
3 points

★ Go to the **railing to the left of the pavilion's main entrance**.

Clue 106: Focus on the side of one of the globes hanging over the lobby to spot another Mickey.
3 points

Clue 107: As you face the entrance from outside, study the mosaic mural on the right wall for a classic Mickey in jewels.
4 points

Clue 108: Outside in front of the pavilion, search for a classic Mickey in the stones embedded in a support for "The Land" sign. (Tip: The support is covered with tiles and stone designs.)
4 points

Clue 109: If you take the "Behind the Seeds" tour, stay alert for a photo of the lettuce classic Mickey that you may have spotted earlier during the ride.
3 points

★ Keep your reservations for dinner. If you don't have reservations, eat at the Food Court in The Land Pavilion.

★ Go to the Imagination! Pavilion and ride **Journey Into Imagination with Figment**.

Clue 110: Squint for a black pair of Mickey ears in the Sight Room.
4 points

Clue 111: Look up at Figment's bathtub for a classic Mickey.
3 points

Clue 112: Now look up again in Figment's bathroom for another classic Mickey near the bathtub.
3 points

Clue 113: Find a classic Mickey on a cloud in the rainbow room.
3 points

Clue 114: Look for a classic Mickey on the wall along the exit hallway.
3 points

★ When you reach **ImageWorks** . . .

Clue 115: Look down inside for a classic Mickey.
4 points

★ Now cross through Innoventions West and head for **Spaceship Earth**. Line up for the ride.

Clue 116: During the ride, keep alert for classic Mickey light patterns on the floor to your right.
5 points

Clue 117: During the ride, notice the Hidden Mickey on the document in front of the sleeping monk.
4 points

Clue 118: In the Renaissance section, spot the classic Mickey formed by paint circles on a tabletop near a painter. (Psst! Look quickly to your left.)
4 points

Clue 119: Look for a chalkboard with the name of a famous Mickey Mouse cartoon.
4 points

Clue 120: Search for Mickey on a car.
4 points

Clue 121: After you exit the ride vehicle, look up for Mickey in the "Project Tomorrow" area.
3 points

★ Cross back through the Innoventions buildings to the **Universe of Energy**. Find a Hidden Mickey as you take in the show and ride.

Clue 122: After the dinosaur section of the ride, watch the movie and look for the shadow of Disney's Hollywood Studios' "Earful" Tower (the tower with Mickey ears) in the door of a church in the background.
5 points

★ Walk **inside Innoventions East**. (Note: Exhibits and attractions inside the Innoventions pavilions change periodically).

Clue 123: Visit the "Don't Waste It!" attraction and spot a classic Mickey in the recycled material.
3 points

★ Look around for a restaurant nearby.

82

Clue 124: Spot Mickey on a menu.
3 points

★ Go to the **Mouse Gear shop**, where you'll find a number of Hidden Mickeys and décor Mickeys.

Clue 125: Before you enter, find the classic Mickey in the sign above the shop entrance.
1 point

★ Now step inside, and keep your eyes peeled.

Clue 126: Examine the nuts on the display racks' bolts.
1 point

Clue 127: Then look for classic Mickeys at the ends of the display racks.
1 point

Clue 128: Now check out the bolt ends themselves.
2 points

Clue 129: Observe the gauges on the wall.
1 point

Clue 130: Search for Donald's shadow.
3 points

Clue 131: Spot a set of Hidden Mickey gears.
2 points

Clue 132: Can you find an image of Donald Duck with a classic Mickey on him?
2 points

Clue 133: Finally, look at the tops of the garment display mannequins.
1 point

★ Walk outside the shop toward *Test Track* and take the first right onto a **walkway leading to World Showcase**.

Clue 134: Stare at the cement as you walk until you discover a Hidden Mickey.
5 points

★ Now cross to the west side of Innoventions Plaza to **Club Cool**.

83

Clue 135: At the front entrance, look near the outside sign for Mickey.
3 points

Clue 136: Search inside Club Cool for a classic Mickey in the interior design.
3 points

Clue 137: Spot Mickey outside at the rear entrance.
3 points

★ Walk past Fountainview Ice Cream to **Epcot Character Spot** and then walk on through the front entrance.

Clue 138: Look above the entrance doors for a Hidden Mickey.
3 points

Clue 139: Search for Mickey's hat in four different places in and around *Epcot Character Spot*.
5 points for spotting all four

Clue 140: Find Goofy and his Hidden Mickey.
3 points

Clue 141: Look around for a yellow classic Mickey made of buttons.
3 points

Clue 142: Don't miss a classic Mickey on a gray metal device.
3 points

Clue 143: Now find Mickey wearing earphones.
2 points

Clue 144: Spot Mickey's gloves.
2 points

Clue 145: Don't miss Mickey in the stars!
3 points

Clue 146: Find Mickey's ears.
1 point

Clue 147: Search for Mickey in the clouds.
3 points

★ Stroll inside Innoventions West to the **"Where's the Fire?"** attraction.

Clue 148: Look for Mickey in the logo.
3 points

Clue 149: Stare at a computer monitor screen.
3 points

Clue 150: Search for a classic Mickey near books.
2 points

Clue 151: Don't forget Goofy! (Tip: He's upside down.)
4 points

Clue 152: Study your **Epcot Guidemap** for a tiny Hidden Mickey.
4 points

## Total Points for Epcot =

### How'd you do?
Up to 203 points - Bronze
204 - 405 points - Silver
406 points and over - Gold
507 points - Perfect Score

If you earned bonus points in the *Test Track* photo selection area, in China, or outside the miniature train exhibit in Germany, you may have done even better!

# Notes

**Caution:
Don't peek at this
section unless you
really want help!**

## The Land Pavilion

### -Soarin'

Hint 1: Along the right side of the entrance queue, five screens show changing artistic landscapes. In the landscape with the purple mountain ridge in the lower background, a large green tree halfway up the right side of the screen hosts a classic Mickey group of flowers.

Hint 2: In the pre-show video, a man who is wearing Mickey Mouse ears is asked to take them off.

Hint 3: In the pre-show video, a boy sitting in his ride seat is wearing a red shirt with a Grumpy logo and shorts sporting Mickey Mouse.

Hint 4: On the ride, when you soar over the hills and spot a golf course, look immediately to your lower left and find a golf cart. The man standing on the other side of the cart is holding a blue Mickey balloon.

Hint 5: Now look to the right side of the golf course. About halfway along the fairway is a slightly distorted shadow classic Mickey on the green grass formed by a cluster of three trees. The "ears" of the shadow Mickey touch the right side of the white cart path.

Hint 6: Look straight ahead and then down to the golf course. Spot the man who is about to swing a golf club. When he strikes the golf ball, it will head directly toward you. Watch the ball's rotation to see the dark classic Mickey on the surface of the ball.

Hint 7: As you complete your *Soarin'* ride over Disneyland, the second burst of fireworks forms a huge classic Mickey in the sky.

## Mission: SPACE

Hint 8: On the far right and left (outer) video monitors in the Mission Control room, classic Mickey circles appear on the lower part of the surface of Mars.

Hint 9: Continue to watch the video loops as three "status lights" form a classic Mickey at the lower right side of the rightmost monitor screen.

Hint 10: During the video loop on either of the middle monitors, three small waveform images merge into a classic Mickey on the lower left of the screen.

Hint 11: You'll see identical faint classic Hidden Mickeys above a horizontal bar on both sides of the launch door before it opens and before you see the sky.

Hint 12: As your spacecraft is landing on Mars, look sharp for a classic Mickey made of satellite dishes on top of the second building from the end, on the right side of the landing strip.

Hint 13: In the Expedition Mars section of the exit exhibit area, you'll find small classic Mickeys in the design of the video-game joystick consoles at the upper left and upper right corners.

Hint 14: In the center of the gift shop near the exit doors, a large side profile of Mickey Mouse is painted on the ceiling in the middle square.

Hint 15: On either side of Mickey's side profile on the ceiling are side profiles of Donald Duck and Pluto (or is it Goofy?).

Hint 16: On the right side of the mural behind the gift shop's cash register, the three round thrusters behind the blue X-2 spaceship form an upside-down classic Mickey.

Hint 17: Look for Minnie Mouse in the same mural. There's a small classic Mickey in the dirt under her left foot.

Hint 18: On the left side of the mural behind the gift shop's cash register, you'll find an upside-down classic Mickey on the lower part of the moon.

Hint 19: The bases of some of the merchandise stands near the gift shop exit contain "support arches" in the shape of Mickey.

Hint 20: You can spot Hidden Mickeys in the electrical tubing on the wall on both sides of the exit door from the gift shop. There's a classic Mickey on one side and both a classic Mickey and a side-profile Mickey on the other.

### -In the entrance plaza

Hint 21: Spot three craters that approximate a classic Mickey at the upper left of the Luna 8 landing site on the back side of the moon.

Hint 22: In the middle of a blue tile area, very near and to the left of a gold strip (as you face the attraction), you'll find a tiny tile classic Mickey (black head and blue ears).

Hint 23: A small classic Mickey formed of white tiles is toward the bottom of a blue tile stripe. Look for a gray disc in the cement, near the lowest part of the stripe. Mickey is hiding about four feet from the disc as you go toward the Mars planet.

Hint 24: Two more tile or stone classic Mickeys (black head and white ears) lie next to a drain cover. Look for the cover in a circle of tiles to the left of the *Mission: SPACE* sign.

## Test Track

### *-In the waiting queue*

Hint 25: Across from area 10a, look for a red tool cabinet. A mug on top of it has a Pez dispenser with a Mickey Mouse head. This Mickey can be spotted best from the Standby and Single Rider queues.

Hint 26: As the queue lines climb toward the pre-show room (and before you get to it), a white "Crash Test Vehicle" in area 5b sports a small inspection sticker. (It's visible from the Single Rider and FASTPASS queues.) The sticker, signed by "M. Mouse," is on the front passenger door.

Hint 27: Near knee calibration area 7b, on the left side of the queue, three washers at the edge of a desk (left of center of the desktop) form an upside-down classic Mickey. This image (and the two following images) can best be seen from the FASTPASS and Single Rider queues.

Hint 28: In the first pre-show room (the Single Riders' room), an orange classic Mickey is on a greaseboard titled "Test Area Notes."

Hint 29: On the lower right side of the bulletin board (next to the greaseboard) in the Single Riders' pre-show room, the front tire of a diagrammed car has Mickey ears.

Hint 30: In the third (farthest away) pre-show room for the Standby queue line, a classic Mickey is formed by a small rectangle and two squares at the upper left of a greaseboard.

### *-During the ride*

Hint 31: As you leave the hot room (the

first environmental chamber), a classic Mickey is drawn or traced on the back side of the round thermometer hanging above you to the right.

Hint 32: During the "Environmental Test" part of the *Test Track* ride, in the second window of the first office to the right of the ride vehicle, a mug contains a pencil with a classic Mickey outline at the top.

Hint 33: In the first "Environmental Test" office, a classic Mickey drawn with a red Magic Marker appears on the lower part of a greaseboard on the rear wall. From time to time, you may be able to spot more than one classic Mickey on this board.

Hint 34: As you enter the cold room, a white classic Mickey is high up way back on the left side of the rear wall (not the left side wall, but the rear wall that you just came through). You must look back to see it.

Hint 35: In the second window of the second "Environmental Test" office to the right of the ride vehicle, a Mickey Mouse plush doll is sitting with its back against the window.

Hints 36 & 37: Just past the office, you have to look quickly to the right, then to the left as you enter the "Corrosion Chamber" to spot two classic Mickeys on auto parts that are just inside the room. Look for a hanging car door to the right and a truck fender to the left. Both sport classic Mickey rust spots.

Hint 38: As you approach the crash barrier wall, a white car (to the left of and facing the ride vehicle) has a classic Mickey on its open gas tank door. It is formed by three crash-test stickers.

Hint 39: Just before the crash barrier wall, look to the floor on your left to try to spot hoses coiled to form a classic Mickey. This Hidden Mickey is hard to spot because you are moving so fast. But you can see it on the *Test Track* photo monitors (see below) if you miss it during the ride.

### -After the ride

Hint 40: At the *Test Track* photo selection area, check the monitors to see the hoses coiled like classic Mickeys. You'll find them in the upper right area of the photos. If the hoses are not visible on the video monitors, check out the framed photo on the wall just before the photo viewing area.

Bonus Points Hint: Also on the *Test Track* monitors, you can sometimes spot a car tire and two hubcaps forming a classic Mickey on the floor behind the car.

Hint 41: Just past the photo viewing area and across from the Die Press is Mickey's face on a sticker on the second locker from the left.

Hint 42: In the last red locker on the right, a worn nametag for "John" has Mickey's shoes and red shorts still visible. The tag is on the top shelf of the locker, in the lap of a white teddy bear wearing sunglasses.

## The Seas with Nemo & Friends Pavilion

### -Turtle Talk with Crush

Hint 43: Look closely at the middle left side of the rear screen, near the edge, to spot a classic Mickey made of coral circles on the rock. Mickey's ears are angled to the left.

## Imagination! Pavilion

### -Captain EO

Hint 44: In the movie, the three lower thrusters on the back of Captain EO's spaceship form a classic Hidden Mickey.

## Odyssey Center

**92**

Hint 45: In the Odyssey Center building, classic Mickeys are in the carpet inside the doors that are nearest the bridge to the *Test Track* area. The largest circles are the "heads," and the smaller circles next to them form the "ears" of classic Mickeys.

## Norway Pavilion

### -Maelstrom

Hint 46: On the left side of the large loading area mural, a Viking in a ship wears Mickey ears. He's sitting below the middle red stripe of the sail.

Hint 47: Toward the right side of the same mural, a woman cruise director holds a clipboard. To the left of the top of her clipboard, the creases in her white shirt form a side profile of Mickey's face. His face is slightly distorted and he's looking to your left.

Hint 48: On the ride as your boat is going backwards, just after you pass a huge polar bear on your left, you will pass through a rock archway. As your boat comes out from under it, stare at the archway. Leaves near the end of a vine on the left middle of the arch cast a classic Mickey shadow on the rock below the vine.

Hint 49: Toward the end of the movie after the *Maelstrom* ride, a red Mickey balloon floats on the right side of the screen. The single balloon is visible above the trees for a few seconds as the movie camera pans down a street filled with parade celebrants.

## Mexico Pavilion

### -Gran Fiesta Tour
### Starring the Three Caballeros

Hint 50: At the beginning of the boat ride, smoke rises from the volcano. Every half minute or so, holes in the smoke form classic Mickeys that quickly disappear.

Hint 51: Along the left wall inside the first tunnel, look at the fourth man from the end.

He is wearing green shorts and has a partially covered blue classic Mickey on the front of his necklace.

Hint 52: Watch for a video screen to the right of your boat that shows a broad expanse of water in the foreground and, in the background, a shoreline edged with modern buildings set against the backdrop of a mountain. Donald Duck is parasailing over the water, but you want to focus on the buildings on the shoreline. One building on the right side of the scene has a dark classic Mickey tree in front of it.

Hint 53: About halfway through the ride, in the small blue pond to the left of the boat, classic Mickeys appear in the bubbles after Donald is taken away. Look above and also to the lower left of the octopus.

Hint 54: Toward the end of the ride, as you enter the fireworks room, three drums form a classic Hidden Mickey at the lower right of the "Viva Donald" barge to the left of your boat.

### -San Angel Inn restaurant

Hint 55: Smoke rising from the volcano by the river forms classic Mickeys that quickly disappear.

## China Pavilion

Hint 56: Classic Mickey-shaped flowers are sculpted on the bases of several decorative light posts on the outside front of the pavilion.

Bonus Points Hint: In the ponds, the floating lily pads sometimes come together to form recognizable classic Mickeys.

## Outpost between China and Germany

Hint 57: At the Outpost, three of the short wooden posts at the corner closest to the bridge form a classic Mickey.

## Germany Pavilion

Hint 58: On the second floor of the building to your right, to the right of the glockenspiel clock, are three suits of armor. The one closest to the glockenspiel has a classic Mickey on its crown.

Hint 59: In the rear of the courtyard, a three-circle classic Mickey formation is in the ironwork support behind the bell on the front of the clock tower.

Hint 60: At the left of the entrance to the Biergarten Restaurant, you can see a wrought iron lion behind a lamp on the outside wall. The lion's front and rear paws are resting on an upside down classic Mickey.

### -Around the miniature train exhibit

Hint 61: Near the small town at the front of the exhibit, look for a shrub shaped like a classic Mickey. It's planted close to the center walkway, which separates the small town from the background of streams, etc.

## Italy Pavilion

Hint 62: In the wine shop, Enoteca Castello, classic Mickeys appear in the woodwork along the relief design of the upper front counter.

Hint 63: A classic Mickey impression is on the left side of the rock wall behind the statue on the right side of the walkway in front of the restaurants.

Hint 64: In the waiting room of Tutto Italia Ristorante, the scrollwork at the middle bottom of the mirror frame forms a classic Mickey.

## The American Adventure Pavilion

Hint 65: A picture on a first-floor wall at the right rear of the rotunda (indoors) shows workers building a skyscraper. The tops of two vertical beams behind the workers sport classic Mickeys.

Hint 66: On the rear wall of the rotunda, first and second floors, large bronze eagle reliefs have classic Mickeys in the corners.

### -The American Adventure show

Hint 67: At the beginning of the film, a classic Mickey appears on the rock behind (and to your right of) a kneeling female pilgrim.

Hint 68: Early in the show, a classic Mickey lock hangs on the right side of a stockade in a scene of the American Revolution time period.

Hint 69: At the end of the show, fireworks light up the sky behind the Statue of Liberty Torch as it rises from the floor. One of the last fireworks at the upper right fizzles into a classic Mickey head (best seen from the right side of the theater).

### -Fife and Drums Corps

Hint 70: Four classic Mickeys appear on the Fife and Drums Corps drums. A black one is on the lower front of the big bass drum. Three more decorate the smaller snare drum: two black (one on each side of the lower part of the drum) and a small blue one (traced on a blue banner on the right rear middle).

## Japan Pavilion

Hint 71: In the koi fish pond across from the Mitsuko-shi store, a drain cover in the water near the bamboo fence sports a classic Mickey.

Hint 72: The trees in the courtyard are encircled by metal grates with classic Mickey designs.

Hint 73: At the rear of the Yakitori House, near the drinking fountain in the outdoor seating area, three short bamboo poles form a classic Mickey when viewed from above.

Hint 74: A classic Mickey formed by three rocks is deep inside a hole in a large bush. It's on the right side of the pavilion, next to the far right sidewalk to the Mitsukoshi store, and near a juniper tree.

## Morocco Pavilion

Hint 75: Three brass plates are arranged to form a classic Mickey on the left green door at the entrance to the Souk-Al-Magreb "Gifts of Morocco" shop on the promenade. (Sometimes, the plates are on the nearby red door.)

Hint 76: You'll find a black classic Mickey on both sides of the red-and-green design on the lower part of the fabric cover atop the Souk-Al-Magreb "Gifts of Morocco" shop. (Note: The fabric cover is sometimes removed temporarily.)

Hint 77: Across from Restaurant Marrakesh, three small classic Mickeys are on a mural on the rear wall of a small room. One is at the top of a tower on the right side of the mural's street. Another is on the left side of the street, next to a double archway. The third is a tiny black Mickey in an upper doorway on the left middle part of the mural.

## France Pavilion

Hint 78: The trees in the courtyard are encircled by metal grates with classic Mickey patterns.

Hint 79: In the patterned hedge (parterre) garden, a bush in the middle right area (on the side nearest the canal) is trimmed to the shape of a classic Mickey.

Hint 80: Classic Mickey images are high on the outside molding of Les Vins de France shop, near the entrance to *Impressions de France*.

Hint 81: Inside Les Vins de France, a small plush figure of Remy (the rat from the movie *Ratatouille*) sits in a basket on a shelf near the ceiling, behind the service counter.

### *-Impressions de France*

Hint 82: In the movie's outdoor wedding scene, you can see a Mickey head and ears in a second floor window of the house in the background. It's in the center screen.

## United Kingdom Pavilion

Hint 83: Outside the Sportsman's Shoppe, a sign has a classic Mickey with a tennis racket head, a soccer ball for one ear and a rugby ball for the other.

Hint 84: In The Crown & Crest Shoppe, you'll find three Mickey stickers inside merchandise cabinets. In each case, you will have to put your head inside the cabinet to spot the Mickey sticker. So please be careful that you don't knock over any merchandise while you're searching. We want these images to hang around awhile.

The first Hidden Mickey is stuck to the wood of the cabinet that's just inside the shop's entrance door and immediately to your right as you enter from outside. This black classic Mickey is taped to the back center of the cabinet's upper horizontal header (the fascia board). Stick your head inside the cabinet (Careful of the merchandise!) and look up and back to find Mickey.

A second Hidden Mickey sticker (this one a full-body Mickey) is in the cabinet immediately to the left of the door. Again, you must put your head inside and look up and back behind the center of the fascia board.

You'll find a third Hidden Mickey on a cabinet to the left of the cash register. He's on the back of the cabinet's support post. Stick your head inside the cabinet and look around the post. Mickey is facing the wall.

## Canada Pavilion

Hint 85: Past the steps into the pavilion, the left totem pole has black classic Mickeys on both sides near the top by the raven's beak.

Hint 86: A small black classic Mickey is on the side of a fish, which is hanging on the outside of a box at the left rear of the first room as you enter the Northwest Mercantile shop.

Hint 87: Behind the check-in desk at Le Cellier Steakhouse, three horizontal bottles

at the center top of a wine display form a classic Mickey.

## Showcase Plaza

### -Disney Traders store

Hint 88: Mickey can be seen running around the equator of the globe that's hanging from the ceiling of Disney Traders (one of the two stores at the front of Showcase Plaza).

## The Seas with Nemo & Friends Pavilion

Hint 89: On the ride, a classic Mickey impression in rock lies below the fifth video screen from the start. It's slightly above and between two pink clusters of standing corals, to the right of center in the rock ledge.

Hint 90: A classic Mickey formed of rocks is at the bottom of the aquarium. It's best seen from the fourth window on the right as you enter the corridor leading to the circular viewing area upstairs. (Warning: this rock Mickey may change locations on the aquarium floor. You may need to look through several windows in the observation area to find it.)

Hint 91: In the manatee viewing room, lower level, bubbles in wall paintings form two classic Mickeys. One is on the left wall (as you exit), in the left middle square containing the words "Manatee Zone ... Slow Speed." Another is on the right wall as you exit, in the lower left square with the polar bear.

Hint 92: As you enter Bruce's room on the lower level, an oyster containing three pearls arranged as a classic Mickey is at the lower right of the second window on the right (labeled "Did You Know?"). A similar oyster with classic Mickey pearls is in the second window on the left (labeled "Bruce's Scrapbook").

Hint 93: In the waiting room for *Turtle Talk with Crush*, a tiny classic Mickey is in the pink and brown coral in the first window painting to the right as you enter the room. At the lower part of the painting, the Mickey is left of the third tallest (leftmost) blue tube, about one quarter of the distance up the side of the tube.

Hint 94: Bubbles come together to form several classic Mickeys on the garbage cans you see in the pavilion.

# The Land Pavilion

### -Living with the Land

Hint 95: In the middle section of the giant wall mural at the rear of the queue, bubbles align to form a classic Mickey, ears angled to the left.

Hint 96: A classic Mickey is formed by shrubs (the "head" has yellow dots on it) to the right of the brim of the farmer's hat near the top of the loading dock mural.

Hint 97: In the lower right area of the mural behind the boat loading area, three circles form a small classic Mickey (a purple circle forms the head and blue circles form the ears). The head is tilted slightly to the right.

Hint 98: In the first part of the ride, a female Cast Member on the last video screen on your left has a Mickey Mouse face hiding on the upper left part of her nametag.

Hint 99: A green garden hose is coiled into a classic Mickey to the right of the boat about halfway through the fish farming section. (Cast Members usually place this Mickey image every morning.)

Hint 100: A classic Mickey made of wire mesh can be found in the aquaculture section, in the freshwater shrimp tube on the right side of the boat.

Hint 101: Plants of different colors are usually arranged to form classic Mickeys in the greenhouses. Often the plants are lettuces.

Hint 102: Toward the end of the ride, a large circular test tube holder on the right side of a "Biotechnology Lab" room has a green classic Mickey head in the center.

Hint 103: On a table toward the left side of this biotech lab, a sign advertises the plant product, "Mickey's Mini Gardens."

### -The Garden Grill Restaurant

Hint 104: On the left side of the large wall mural of vegetation is a Mickey hiding behind the most prominent fern that extends all the way to the top. Counting up horizontally from the bottom of the fern, his face is mostly behind the fifth through eighth leaves on the fern's right side. He's looking slightly downward and to the right in a three-quarter profile. Two black circles that form his eyes are visible above the sixth fern leaf on the right, more than halfway to the end of the leaf. Mickey's ears jut above the seventh leaf, and his mouth and nose are below the sixth leaf. His face and ears are green, and his mouth is slightly open. This Hidden Mickey is a real classic!

Hint 105: In the restaurant, Chip 'n' Dale wear red bandannas with small, dark classic Mickeys in the design.

### -Main entrance to The Land Pavilion

Hint 106: From the upper level railing, just to the left as you walk in the main entrance, a classic Mickey is on the Earth above the lobby. It's in water swirls, to the left of the tip of South America.

Hint 107: A classic Mickey is in the mosaic mural on the right wall outside as you enter The Land Pavilion. Find the word "LAND" on the mural and look slightly above and to the right about six feet or so to a reddish plateau. Just above the left side of the flat upper part of the plateau are three jewels, a green "head" and two reddish "ears."

Hint 108: The Land Pavilion sign outside the entrance rests on two large stone- and tile-covered supports. On the end of the right-hand support, embedded stones decorate the upper portion of the green-tiled area. A small classic Mickey, formed of three stones, lies near the center of the stone decoration.

Hint 109: About halfway along the "Behind the Seeds" tour in the greenhouses, an electrical box on the right side of the tour path sports a photo of a lettuce classic Mickey. You may have spotted one similar to it during the *Living with the Land* ride; see clue and hint 101.

## Imagination! Pavilion

### -Journey Into Imagination with Figment

Hint 110: In the center of the Sight Room, headphones on the left of two tables have Mickey ears on an earpiece!

Hint 111: Three bubbles make a classic Mickey near Figment's hand on the edge of his bathtub.

Hint 112: In Figment's Upside-Down House, his toilet forms a classic Mickey with two red circles on the floor.

Hint 113: When you feel a blast of air and the walls open, you'll see a rainbow and balloons. Look down and to the right to see classic Mickey circles appear on a cloud at the bottom right of the stage

Hint 114: On the left wall of the exit hallway, a sideways classic Mickey is behind and between the "I" and "m" of the *ImageWorks* sign.

### -ImageWorks

Hint 115: Behind a pillar in the middle of *ImageWorks*, a classic Hidden Mickey is on the floor made of tan-colored tile.

# Spaceship Earth

Hint 116: After the fall of Rome, you see three Islamic scholars seated around a table on the floor. They are illuminated by lights that form patterns on the floor. The outer circle of light patterns form classic Mickeys.

Hint 117: During the ride, in a scene to the left, monks are writing at desks. In front of the sleeping monk is a document with a small ink blot at the upper right corner. The blot is shaped like a classic Mickey and becomes visible as your vehicle passes by.

Hint 118: Just after the Gutenberg printing press scene, in the first part of the Renaissance section, look for the first painter to the left of your ride vehicle. Three white paint circles form a classic Mickey on the top left of the table near the painter. You have to look fast for this one.

Hint 119: On the right side, as you're passing the section showing black and white movies, a chalkboard marquee on the ground lists upcoming features. One is "The Band Concert," a famous Mickey Mouse cartoon.

Hint 120: Just past the large computer room, a Mickey Mouse sticker is on the bottom left of the rear window, driver's side, of a red car to the left of the ride vehicle.

Hint 121: At the exit of *Spaceship Earth*, several classic Mickeys float along on overhead blue screens in the Project Tomorrow interactive area.

# Universe of Energy

Hint 122: After the dinosaur section of the ride, the movie shows a man driving a car out of a barn and towards a church building in the background (the fourth building from the left). A shadow of the Disney's Hollywood Studios' "Earful" Tower appears in the door of the church.

# Innoventions

### -"Don't Waste It!" in Innoventions East

Hint 123: In the "Don't Waste It!" attraction, a classic Mickey image is at the bottom of the metal recycling display, on the side facing toward the plastic and glass recycling displays.

### -Electric Umbrella in Innoventions East

Hint 124: Look for a menu outside or inside the restaurant. An apple between "Kids'" and "Picks" has a classic Mickey image formed by bites out of the apple. This "Kids' Picks" apple image is found at many restaurants around Walt Disney World.

### -Mouse Gear shop in Innoventions Plaza

Hint 125: The signs above the shop entrances have classic Mickeys with two round ears above the letter "G" as the head.

Hint 126: The large wing nuts on the bolts of the display racks form Mickey ears.

Hint 127: At the ends of some of the display racks, bolts next to larger holes form classic Mickeys.

Hint 128: The ends of some of the large bolts that jut out from the stippled panels on the merchandise cases are stamped with classic Mickeys.

Hint 129: Some of the gauges on the wall are arranged as classic Mickeys.

Hint 130: The shadows of Donald Duck and his relatives are on the upper part of a wall in the center of the store.

Hint 131: Classic Mickey gears hang above a display on a wall opposite the cash registers.

Hint 132: Look for a large Donald Duck on a wall in the part of the store near the main walkway to the east side of Future World to find a classic Mickey made of gears.

Hint 133: Some of the garment display manne-quins have classic Mickeys at the top.

Hint 134: Outside and behind Mouse Gear is a classic Mickey in the walkway cement. Exit the shop at the rear heading toward *Test Track*, then take the first right onto a walkway (heading toward World Showcase). Just before the path changes to an octagonal shape, look down near the left railing to find a small classic Mickey in-dented in the concrete.

### -Club Cool near Innoventions West

Hint 135: Holes in the metal bracket supports be-hind the outdoor sign form classic Mickeys.

Hint 136: Above you, on a colorful decorative border in the middle of the club, green circles form an upside-down classic Mickey.

Hint 137: A classic Mickey is near the bottom of the blue banners that are located outside and above the rear entrance to Club Cool.

### -Epcot Character Spot

Hint 138: A small white classic Mickey is on the inside wall among the stars above the entrance doors to the *Character Spot*. He's to the upper right of the exit sign.

Hint 139: A Mickey hat appears in several places: near the right end of the inside wall mural in the waiting queue, outside on window murals near the entrance doors and over the exit doors, and on the outdoor sign, where it is behind and below the "CH" on the side of the sign that faces The Land Pavilion.

Hint 140: Goofy is on an upper inside window, across from the second greeting bay. There's a small, white classic Mickey on his spacesuit.

Hint 141: The yellow buttons on a giant cell phone on the right side of the middle greet-ing bay form a classic Mickey.

Hint 142: Behind the giant cell phone, at the right rear of the middle greeting bay, you'll find a classic Mickey on a gray metal device.

Hint 143: At the left rear of the middle greeting bay, a metal 3-D Mickey head wears earphones.

Hint 144: Mickey's gloves are on a robot light switch in the next to last greeting bay.

Hint 145: A constellation classic Mickey is on the right rear wall of the last greeting bay.

Hint 146: In the last bay on the right, a green alien wears Mickey Mouse ears.

Hint 147: A side-profile cloud Mickey floats in the sky mural on an upper inside window across from the last greeting bay.

### -"Where's the Fire?" in Innoventions West

Hint 148: A partial classic Mickey is at the lower left of the "Where's the Fire?" logo, which appears between shows on all the monitors in this attraction.

Hint 149: In one of the rooms, look for a computer monitor screen on a desk. You can make out classic Mickeys in the changing graphics on the screen.

Hint 150: A classic Mickey bookend is visible on the desk in the Kids' Bedroom.

Hint 151: Goofy is on an upside-down magazine draped over a lamp in the Kids' Bedroom.

## Epcot Guidemap

Hint 152: Look under number 5 on the park map (in the Innoventions West building) by the water. At the upper side of the lake, there is a bush or flowerbed shaped like Mickey's head (red and green "head" and green "ears").

# CHAPTER 4

# Disney's Hollywood Studios Scavenger Hunt

Note: Many of the Hidden Mickeys in this park are in restaurants and shops. Be considerate of fellow guests and Cast Members as you search. Tell them what you are looking for, so they can share in the fun. Avoid searching restaurants at busy meal times unless you are one of the diners.

★ Your scavenger hunt in Disney's Hollywood Studios (aka "the Studios") starts even **before you enter the park**.

Clue 1: Look closely at the brackets on the signs above the ticket windows.
2 points

Clue 2: Examine the fence at the entrance turnstiles.
1 point

★ Walk first to *Toy Story Midway Mania!*

Clue 3: Find Mickey on a block outside the entrance.
2 points

Clue 4: Search carefully for a blue classic Mickey along the Standby (i.e., regular) entrance queue.
5 points

Clue 5: As your ride starts, glance back at a big book for Donald and Mickey.
5 points for both

Clue 6: On the interactive screens, look behind the target balloons in front of the volcano for a classic Mickey.
5 points

107

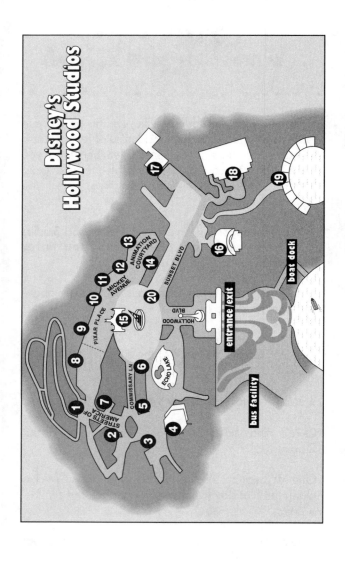

Disney's
Hollywood Studios

1 Lights, Motors, Action!®Extreme Stunt Show

2 MuppetVision 3-D

3 Star Tours

4 Indiana Jones™ Epic Stunt Spectacular!

5 Sounds Dangerous — Starring Drew Carey

6 The American Idol Experience

7 "Honey, I Shrunk the Kids" Movie Set Adventure

8 Studio Backlot Tour

9 Toy Story Midway Mania!™

10 Journey Into Narnia: Prince Caspian

11 Walt Disney: One Man's Dream

12 Voyage of The Little Mermaid

13 The Magic of Disney Animation

14 Disney Junior — Live on Stage!

15 The Great Movie Ride

16 "Beauty and the Beast" — Live on Stage

17 Rock 'n' Roller Coaster® Starring Aerosmith

18 The Twilight Zone Tower of Terror™

19 Fantasmic!

20 Guest Information Board

109

Clue 7: Stay alert for a classic Mickey below an exclamation point on the wall.
5 points

Clue 8: Along the exit walkway, spot another classic Mickey on a wall.
2 points

Clue 9: Study a book along the exit for a tiny classic Mickey.
5 points

Clue 10: Outside of the attraction, look around for popcorn Mickey.
3 points

Clue 11: Then search outside for Mickey on a plate.
2 points

★ Now go to **Rock 'n' Roller Coaster Starring Aerosmith**. (You can find the Hidden Mickeys here without riding the coaster, the first ten by exiting before the ride, two in the gift shop by walking in through the exit from outside, and three outside in the courtyard.)

Clue 12: Look down at the carpet along the entrance queue for Hidden Mickeys.
4 points

Clue 13: Don't miss the tiny Mickey on a wall poster just before the pre-show room.
4 points

Clue 14: Search the pre-show room for a classic Mickey.
4 points

Clue 15: After the pre-show, find three Mickeys on a poster.
4 points for spotting all three

Clue 16: Before boarding, spot two Mickeys near the ceiling.
4 points for spotting both

Clue 17: Look across the track for Mickey on the wall.
5 points

Clue 18: At the loading gate, look at the rear license plates of the limo ride vehicles. (Then exit if you wish.)
4 points

Clue 19: At the exit, find a box with a classic Mickey. (If you haven't taken the ride, walk in through the gift shop to the video monitor area to find this Mickey.)
4 points

Clue 20: In the gift shop, spot Mickey on the wall.
3 points

Clue 21: Outside in the courtyard, search for three Hidden Mickeys on the wall.
5 points for spotting all three

★ Walk to ***The Twilight Zone Tower of Terror*** and explore the entry queue area and pre-show for three Hidden Mickeys.

Clue 22: During the pre-show film in the library, find the plush Mickey Mouse doll held by a little girl.
3 points

Clue 23: Linger in the left library to spot the words "Mickey Mouse" on sheet music on a desktop.
4 points

Clue 24: Notice a classic Mickey stain on the wall in the boiler room.
4 points

(Tip: For the best vantage point for the ride Hidden Mickeys, take the right queue when the line for the ride splits. Then tell the Cast Member you're hunting for Hidden Mickeys and ask to be seated in the right-most ride vehicle.)

Clue 25: At the first stop on the ride, search for a Hidden Mickey above you.
4 points

Clue 26: Also look for a Mickey Mouse doll here.
4 points

Clue 27: Stare at the star field (the doors to the elevator shaft just before they open!) to

spot a classic Hidden Mickey in the stars.
5 points

Clue 28: After you leave your elevator, keep alert for a classic Mickey near the photo selection area.
3 points

Clue 29: As you exit, spot Mickey on the floor!
4 points

Clue 30: Outside the gift shop at the exit, check out the rock wall at the smoking area for a classic Mickey.
4 points

★ Walk down Sunset Boulevard and turn right to **The Great Movie Ride**. First find two classic Mickeys among the celebrity impressions in the cement in front of the Chinese Theater and then take the ride.

(If the wait is more than 15 minutes, go on to *Star Tours: The Adventures Continue* and try *The Great Movie Ride* later. Best times: during a parade or two hours before park closing.)

Clue 31: Check Harry Anderson's square.
3 points

Clue 32: Now see if you can spot a Mickey in Carol Burnett's square.
3 points

Clue 33: In the middle of the loading dock mural, search for the Hidden Minnie above a tree stump. (Psst! It's visible at loading and unloading.)
5 points

Clue 34: On the right side of this mural, squint for a tiny black Hidden Mickey.
5 points

Clue 35: As you start down Gangster Alley, look for Mickey's brown shoes under a James Cagney poster.
4 points

Clue 36: In the "Western" section, spot a reference to Pocahontas.
4 points

Clue 37: At the end of Gangster Alley, find Mickey's shadow in a window near the top of the "Chemical Company" building.
5 points

Clue 38: In the "Raiders of the Lost Ark" scene, stare to the right of your vehicle for a small white classic Mickey on a tablet below the ark container. It's near a snake.
5 points

Clue 39: Find Mickey and Donald on the left wall, at the end of the "Raiders of the Lost Ark" scene. (Psst! Mickey is facing Donald.)
5 points

Clue 40: In the "Tarzan" scene, stare at the trees high above and to your right for a classic Mickey.
3 points

Clue 41: In the "Wizard of Oz" room, search for Mickey in the flowers.
3 points

Clue 42: Look up to spot Mickey in the trees in the "Wizard of Oz" set.
5 points

Clue 43: After you exit, study the design above the outside entrance door for a classic Mickey image.
3 points

★ Outside the exit, walk past the Sorcerer's Hat and turn right (with Echo Lake on your left) to **Star Tours: The Adventures Continue**. You can exit before the ride if you prefer to focus on the scavenger hunt.

(If the line is too long, use the FASTPASS option if it's available to you.)

Clue 44: Don't miss a classic Mickey on a tree along the outside queue.
5 points

Clue 45: Find a classic Mickey in the gift shop at the exit.
3 points

★ Catch the next **Lights, Motors, Action! Extreme Stunt Show**.

Clue 46: Don't miss classic Mickeys along the entrance walkway.
4 points for one or more

Clue 47: Search for a small full-body Mickey Mouse at the rear of the set.
5 points

Clue 48: Find a classic Mickey in a set window.
5 points

Clue 49: Stay alert for fiery Mickey ears.
5 points

★ Take a lunch break. Keep your reservations if you have them. If not, try the Backlot Express for burgers and sandwiches, the Pizza Planet Arcade for pizza, or the ABC Commissary for salads and stir-fry.

★ Check your Times Guide for convenient shows of The American Idol Experience and Beauty and the Beast. While you're seated, **check your Studios Guidemap** for a Hidden Mickey.

Clue 50: Turn the Disney's Hollywood Studios map upside down and search for Mickey.
4 points

Clue 51: Now study the map right side up for tiny side profiles of Mickey and Minnie.
3 points

★ After lunch, go to **MuppetVision 3-D** and find five Hidden Mickeys and a Hidden Surprise.

Clue 52: Look for a Mickey Mouse in the fountain outside MuppetVision.
2 points

Clue 53: On the wall near the far turn of the long outside waiting queue, check out the poster about 3-D glasses to find a classic Mickey.
3 points

Clue 54: During the first part of the pre-show on the video monitors, observe the test pattern.
4 points

Clue 55: Try to spot the Mickey balloons while Kermit rides in on a fire truck.
3 points

Clue 56: Study the license plate on the fire truck for a Hidden Surprise.
4 points

Clue 57: Find a Mickey image just outside the theater exit doors.
3 points

★ Walk up the Streets of America. Turn right and pass by the *"Honey I Shrunk the Kids" Movie Set Adventure* to the **Studio Backlot Tour**.

Clue 58: Don't miss a drawing of Walt Disney and two images of Mickey Mouse on the wall.
3 points for spotting all three images

Clue 59: Search for Mickey's gloves and shoes in the prop storage area.
3 points for spotting both

Clue 60: Look closely at the refrigerator on the right side of the first aisle in the prop storage area.
3 points

Clue 61: Find Mickey and Minnie in the second aisle.
3 points

(Caution: If the waiting queue is short, you may be directed past the winding aisles of the prop storage area. To check out the Hidden Mickeys here, step past the ropes to explore the aisles away from the crowds.)

Clue 62: While on the tram, stay alert for Mickey on the wall of the sewing room to your left.
3 points

Clue 63: While on the tram, spot a classic
Mickey on an airplane.
3 points

Clue 64: Study a mural in the exit displays (after the tram ride) for three Mickey images.
5 points for spotting all three

★ Walk to **Studio Catering Co.**

Clue 65: Search for a Hidden Mickey on a wall.
3 points

★ Walk down Mickey Avenue to **Walt Disney: One Man's Dream**.

Clue 66: During your walk through the attraction, look around for a Hidden Donald near Walt, who is holding a pointer.
3 points

Clue 67: Now find Mickey on the wall near Walt.
3 points

★ Check out the show **Disney Junior – Live on Stage!** in Animation Courtyard.

Clue 68: Watch for Mickey in the lighting and stage effects.
3 points for two or more

★ Continue down Mickey Avenue, then up the steps or through the arch, and veer left to **The Hollywood Brown Derby** restaurant. Admire the mural on the wall outside, above the restaurant.

Clue 69: Look for two classic Mickeys in the mural.
4 points for spotting both

★ Now look at the pictures in the waiting area inside the restaurant.

Clue 70: Spot the man with Mickey Mouse ears.
3 points

★ Catch a performance of **The American Idol Experience**.

Clue 71: Find two Mickeys on the stage backdrop.
5 points each

Clue 72: Watch for a Hidden Mickey in a video of Jordan Sparks.
4 points

★ Turn left as you leave and **head down Sunset Boulevard**.

Clue 73: Search for a classic Mickey in scrollwork on a blue building.
4 points

Clue 74: Look around for Mickey in a café behind the service counter.
3 points

★ Now catch a performance of **Beauty and the Beast**.

Clue 75: Watch for Mickey on the back of one of the characters.
3 points

★ Turn left onto Hollywood Boulevard, then right to **Hollywood & Vine** restaurant.

Clue 76: Seek a Hidden Character above the entrance.
3 points

★ Enter the restaurant and examine the left wall.

Clue 77: Find a stick figure Mickey.
2 points

Clue 78: Search the wall for some classic Mickeys.
3 points

★ Step inside the waiting area for the **50's Prime Time Café** and look closely at the tables.

Clue 79: Check out what's holding them together.
1 point

★ Walk to a faux security booth **near Indiana Jones Epic Stunt Spectacular!**

Clue 80: Find two Mickeys!
4 points for spotting both

★ Enter the **Backlot Express restaurant**.

Clue 81: Look for standing Mickeys.
4 points for finding four or more

★ Stroll to the **Radio Disney sign** to the left of *Sounds Dangerous*.

Clue 82: Take a good look at the "O."
1 point

★ Ask a restaurant Cast Member to let you check out the **Sci-Fi Dine-In Theater Restaurant** inside.

Clue 83: Look for a classic Mickey in the waiting area.
3 points

Clue 84: Find a full-body Mickey in the waiting area.
3 points

Clue 85: Study the right rear mural. Look for Mickey's ears along the treetops. (Psst! They're near a tall palm.)
5 points

Clue 86: Now search for a waving Mickey.
5 points

Clue 87: Stare at a small mosaic mural at the rear of the restaurant for a side profile of Mickey Mouse.
5 points

Clue 88: Watch the movie reel for three Hidden Characters.
8 points for spotting all three

Clue 89: Stay alert for a classic Mickey on a spacesuit.
4 points

Clue 90: Find a Hidden Mickey on a dining car.
3 points

★ Get yourself some coffee or other refreshment at **The Writer's Stop**. Look up while you enjoy it.

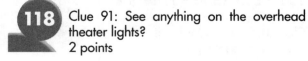

**118**  Clue 91: See anything on the overhead theater lights?
2 points

★ Mosey over to the **Pizza Planet Arcade** and find three Hidden Mickeys.

Clue 92: Search for a small classic Mickey in the stars above the counter registers. Focus on the left side of the pizzeria's rear wall.
4 points

Clue 93: Swing your eyes over to the right side of the rear wall to find a bright classic-Mickey star cluster.
3 points

Clue 94: Now find a three-quarter Mickey profile above the arcade games on the wall mural. (Psst! He's looking left.)
5 points

★ Wander into the **Stage 1 Company Store** and find four Hidden Mickeys.

Clue 95: Locate a classic Mickey near a bird.
2 points

Clue 96: Take a good look at the old bureau that's loaded with hats and paint cans.
3 points

Clue 97: Spot a classic Mickey on the wall.
3 points

Clue 98: Search for some famous shorts.
3 points

★ In the waiting area for **Mama Melrose's Ristorante Italiano**, search for four classic Mickeys.

Clue 99: Check out the Dalmatian.
3 points

Clue 100: Examine the plaster on the right wall.
3 points

Clue 101: Find a classic Mickey leaf near the check-in podium.
4 points

Clue 102: Now look at the plaster on the wall to the left of the check-in podium.
3 points

★ Stroll to **Radiator Springs**, where the *Cars* characters sign autographs.

Clue 103: Study Mater for a Hidden Mickey.
3 points

Clue 104: Spot a side-profile Mickey.
4 points

★ Walk down the **Streets of America**.

Clue 105: Search for a San Francisco newspaper with a Hidden Mickey.
4 points

Clue 106: Keep looking around for a reference to a recent Disney movie.
3 points

Clue 107: Along the street, locate a dog with a Hidden Mickey.
3 points

Clue 108: Find a Mickey Mouse watch in a window.
4 points

Clue 109: Don't miss the photo of Walt with Mickey!
4 points

Clue 110: Search for three classic characters in a window near a cruise ship.
4 points for spotting all three

Clue 111: Spot a classic Mickey in the sand in a New York window.
3 points

★ Walk left to the **end of Commissary Lane**, then stop at a faux security booth labeled "Gate 1."

Clue 112: Find Mickey inside the booth.
2 points

★ Walk past *The Great Movie Ride* to the entrance arch to **Animation Courtyard**.

Clue 113: Search the show's entrance area for Hidden Characters.
4 points for finding two characters

★ Enjoy **The Magic of Disney Animation**.

Clue 114: Look around the stage props in the first theater presentation for Hidden Mickeys.
5 points for four or more

Clue 115: In the first video, watch for Hidden Mickeys on a mug.
4 points

Clue 116: Study the carpets inside the attraction.
2 points

Clue 117: Search all the Character Greeting areas.
5 points for four Hidden Mickeys or more

★ Stroll **toward Hollywood Boulevard**.

Clue 118: On the way, look for Mickey in front of his Sorcerer's Hat.
3 points

Clue 119: At the **intersection of Hollywood and Sunset Boulevards**, discover Mickey Mouse's previous moniker. (Psst! Read the impressions in the sidewalks, near the curb.)
5 points

★ Look at a billboard above **Keystone Clothiers**.

Clue 120: See any handprints in cement?
3 points

Clue 121: Walk behind Keystone Clothiers and search for a classic Mickey.
2 points

Clue 122: Study the outside display windows of **Disney & Company**.
2 points

★ Enter **Mickey's of Hollywood** to look for four Hidden Mickeys.

Clue 123: Check the posts holding up merchandise racks.
2 points

Clue 124: Now examine the racks themselves.
2 points

Clue 125: Study the cabinets in the Sorcerer section of the store. (Tip: They are near a door to the street.)
2 points

Clue 126: Next find "MICKEYS" spelled out on vertical dividers.
1 point

★ Go to the **Cover Story** store and take a good look at the outside.

Clue 127: Can you spot classic Mickeys in the design?
2 points

★ Walk outside the park to the **charter bus area**.

Clue 128: Search the cement next to a bench.
5 points

★ In the evening during the **Fantasmic!** show...

Clue 129: Look for large bubbles floating up the water screen that form a classic Hidden Mickey.
5 points

**Total Points
for Disney's Hollywood Studios =**

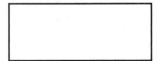

**How'd you do?**

Up to 184 points – Bronze
185 - 368 points – Silver
369 points and over – Gold
461 points - Perfect Score

**Caution:
Don't peek at this
section unless you
really want help!**

### -Park entrance area

Hint 1: Metal brackets at the bottoms of signs above the ticket purchase windows are shaped like classic Mickeys.

Hint 2: You'll see classic Mickeys on top of the fence at the turnstiles.

### -Toy Story Midway Mania!

Hint 3: A classic Mickey is traced onto a "Toy Story 3" wood block, which is in a stack of blocks outside the entrance to the attraction.

Hint 4: An upside-down blue paint classic Mickey is on the wall past the large map of the U.S.A. He is below a green dinosaur and an orange fish (Nemo), near the floor and behind the handrails on the left side of the queue.

Hint 5: Just as your vehicle leaves the loading area, glance back at the large "Tin Toy" book. On the back of the book, near the

**123**

spine, spot full-body images of Donald Duck at the upper right corner and Mickey Mouse two figures below Donald.

Hint 6: Watch for the screen with target balloons in front of the volcano spewing lava. If you pop the middle 100-point balloon on second tier, a light classic Mickey appears on the rear surface in the lava behind the balloons.

Hint 7: Look for the words "Circus Fun!" on the wall to your right as you rotate into position for the last screen stop. The dot below the exclamation point is a classic Mickey.

Hint 8: On the wall to the left of the ride vehicles, a classic Mickey is formed by three ovals that outline Mr. Potato Head, Slinky Dog, and Bullseye the horse. You can see this image at loading and unloading, and you can study it as you take the exit walkway.

Hint 9: On the upper spine of the large "Tin Toy" book along the exit, a tiny white classic Mickey is in a chicken's eye. It's the fourth image from the top of the spine.

Hint 10: You'll find a side-profile Mickey on a huge popcorn box that's on display across from the *Toy Story Midway Mania!* attraction. Look behind the "Hey Howdy Hey!" sign.

Hint 11: On the left lower side of a large "Prospector" plate, which stands on the left side of a rear wall shelf of the "Hey Howdy Hey" snack area, a horseshoe and two circles resemble a classic Mickey.

### -Rock 'n' Roller Coaster Starring Aerosmith

Hint 12: Along the entrance queue, when you reach the inner room past the tile floor, distorted classic Mickeys are in the carpet.

Hint 13: On the last wall before you enter the lower level of the pre-show room, a poster labeled "Cosmic Car Show" has a tiny classic Mickey on the bottom right under the front tire of the car.

Hint 14: Cables coiled into a classic Mickey lie on the rear center of the floor in the pre-show room where Aerosmith appears.

Hint 15: You'll find three full-body Mickey Mouse stickers at the upper right and middle right side of a collage poster. The poster is on the wall to your left, at the first right turn in the inside queue near the boarding area.

Hint 16: After the right turn in the inside queue near the boarding area, about halfway to the end and above the "Compact Vehicles Only" notation on the wall, the first and third light fixtures near the ceiling sport Mickey stickers.

Hint 17: Across from the front of the loading dock area, various items (mostly hats) are hanging from a row of hooks to the left of a wall cabinet and to the right of a garage door. The third hanging item from the right is a pink hat with the word "Mickey" across the front. (Note: The arrangement of these items changes from time to time.)

Hint 18: On the rear license plate of each limo ride vehicle, the year sticker at the upper right is a classic Mickey.

Hint 19: Just as people exit the ride vehicle, look for "Box #15" on the side. The "o" in "Box" is a classic Mickey.

Hint 20: In the gift shop, a shadowbox display on the wall near the exit walkway holds a classic Mickey formed by black disks.

Hint 21: As you exit into the front courtyard, check the outside wall mural to your left for: a boy wearing Mickey ears, black classic Mickeys on a singer's shirt, and a gold "bling" Mickey on the necklace of the man in the black suit.

### -The Twilight Zone Tower of Terror

Hint 22: During the pre-show film in the library, the little girl on the elevator holds a plush Mickey Mouse doll.

Hint 23: Look for sheet music on a desktop and under a trumpet to the right of the television in the left library. The words "Mickey Mouse" are part of a song title: "What! No Mickey Mouse?"

Hint 24: A black, slightly distorted classic Mickey stains the wall of the boiler room at the spot where the queue branches. He's about eight feet up from the walkway, between an "Exit" sign and a red electrical box.

Hint 25: At the first stop on the ride, a small, dark classic Mickey can be seen above the ghostly images in the lower center of the ornate design on the closest archway.

Hint 26: Also at this first stop, the little girl in the ghostly images is still holding her Mickey doll.

Hint 27: On the ride itself, you'll see a bright star field just before the doors open into the elevator shaft. Look closely as the stars you're watching converge in the middle into a small classic Mickey shape for a split second. (Tip: You see it best from the rightmost ride vehicle.)

Hint 28: In the room below and behind the screens that show the photo ride images, look to the left to an open drawer in which gauges form a classic Mickey.

Hint 29: On the left side of the last room as you exit the ride (and before the gift shop), three distinct floor tiles form a classic Mickey. (It's not proportioned correctly but it is clearly purposeful).

Hint 30: In the trellis-covered smoking area across from the gift shop exit, a tiny rock classic Mickey sticks out from the last arch on the left of the upper rear rock wall. It's about four feet from the end column and close to the bottom of the arch.

### -The Great Movie Ride

Hint 31: Harry Anderson's celebrity impression is at the front left of the Chinese Theater (as you face the entrance). Look for a classic Mickey on Harry's tie.

Hint 32: Four squares to the right of Harry Anderson's impression, Carol Burnett's square has classic Mickey ears in the upper right side.

Hint 33: In the loading dock area, a shadow of Minnie Mouse's head in side profile is visible on the wall mural during loading and unloading. To find it, first spot the house in the middle of the mural. Then look above and to the right of the house to spot Minnie's shadow. She's looking to your left. Having trouble? Look at the ride vehicles. The Minnie shadow is to the left of the front section of the second of the two vehicles.

Hint 34: On the right side of the loading dock mural, a tiny black classic Mickey is in the bottom center of a top-floor window on the side of the house nearest the corner. It's the second to last house on the right.

Hint 35: In the first part of Gangster Alley, Mickey Mouse's brown shoes and tail poke out from under a James Cagney poster, "The Public Enemy," on the left side of the ride vehicle.

Hint 36: At the end of Gangster Alley, a silhouette of Mickey in side profile appears in the rightmost window, near the top of the "Chemical Company" building. It's to the rear left of your ride vehicle.

Hint 37: To the left of your vehicle, just past John Wayne, one of the paper bulletins on the wood fence advertises "Pocahontas Remedies." It's one of the lower bulletins, toward the right of the collection of bulletins.

Hint 38: In the "Raiders of the Lost Ark" scene, a small white classic Mickey is on a broken tablet (or flat rock) that leans against the foundation the Ark container is sitting on. Two white men are painted on the side of the container, and the Mickey image is below and between them. It's just to the left of the head of an orange-brown snake.

Hint 39: On the left wall, at the end of the "Raiders of the Lost Ark" scene, Mickey and Donald can be found in the far left corner of the scene. They're facing one another and Mickey is to the right of Donald, on the third row of panes up from the floor.

Hint 40: In the latter part of the "Tarzan" scene, a basket high in a treehouse to the right contains three eggs that form a classic Mickey. (The eggs are all the same size, but this is a sentimental favorite Hidden Mickey among guests and Cast Members).

Hint 41: In the "Wizard of Oz" set, several groups of flowers, among them three large blue flowers above a hut at the middle left of the room, form acceptable classic Mickeys.

Hint 42: A classic Mickey is nestled in the top of the trees, midway along the mural above the exit from the "Wizard of Oz" room. The classic Mickey is tilted slightly to the right.

Hint 43: Near the top of the flames directly above the small gold statue that is standing over the entrance doors to the attraction, a red circle with swirls for ears resembles a classic Mickey.

### -Star Tours: The Adventures Continue

Hint 44: About halfway along the outside winding queue for *Star Tours*, a white classic Mickey is high on a tree trunk, just below the walkway platform for the Ewok village above. It's on the huge central tree, directly across from the Imperial Walker.

Hint 45: At the "Build Your Own Lightsaber" station in the shop at the exit, a classic Mickey is on the front lower right panel. It's formed by bullet holes with surrounding black burn marks as the "ears" and a central raised circle as the "head."

### -Lights, Motors, Action! Extreme Stunt Show

Hint 46: Walk through the entrance turnstile and look through the windows of the building on your right. Classic Mickey magnets are stuck on red tool chests behind the first set of windows you encounter and behind the middle set of windows as you turn right at the first corner. These magnet Mickeys change positions on the tool chests at times.

Hint 47: In the right section of the set background, look for a window under an "Antiquities" sign and near a large "Café" sign. A full-body drawing of Mickey Mouse is near a chair in the window's lower right side.

Hint 48: A classic Mickey is behind the upper right windowpane at the rear of the set, under the sign "Motomania."

Hint 49: Near the end of the show, a fireball erupts at the front center of the stage set ("downstage center" in stage parlance). The fire forms Mickey ears for a split second.

### -Disney's Hollywood Studios Guidemap

Hint 50: The face of Mickey Mouse on the upside-down park map has been distorted over time. The corners of his smile are still visible on both sides of the big Sorcerer's Hat, and his forehead "widow's peak" shows up just below where Hollywood Boulevard ends. (Look closely and you'll see that his smile and widow's peak are darker areas in the cement.) To the right, Echo Lake forms a distorted ear.

Hint 51: On the rightside-up map, a filmstrip flowerbed adorns the right side of the entrance plaza in front of the trees. A green side profile of Mickey is in the fourth square from the bottom of the filmstrip. He's looking at Minnie, who is in the third square from the bottom.

### -MuppetVision 3-D

Hint 52: In a fountain outside *MuppetVision 3-D*, Gonzo is balancing on a character with bulging eyes and face who resembles Mickey.

Hint 53: On the wall near the far turn of the long outside waiting queue, you'll find

129

a classic Mickey in the center left of a blue poster that says, "5 reasons to return . . . 3-D glasses."

Hint 54: During the first part of the pre-show on the video monitors, a test pattern appears after you see the words "Video Display Test." The black lines on a white background form a classic Hidden Mickey.

Hint 55: After the cannon shoots holes in the theater and Kermit rides in on a fire truck, you can see that some of the observers outside are holding Mickey Mouse balloons.

Hint 56: An image of Cinderella Castle (a Hidden Surprise) is on a license plate at the right lower corner of the fire truck Kermit is riding.

Hint 57: Across from and outside the exit doors from the *MuppetVision 3D* theater, a poster on the right wall advertises "Rowlf." At the lower left of the poster, a classic Mickey is formed by the nose and eyes of the dog's face.

### -Studio Backlot Tour

Hint 58: An advertisement with Walt Disney and Mickey Mouse is on a bulletin board behind glass, on the right side of the entrance walkway into the props area. It's in the third display board from the entrance doors. A drawing of Mickey is in the same display, to the left of the purple image of Walt and Mickey.

Hint 59: Along the first aisle, straight ahead in the prop storage building, you'll find Mickey's gloves and then his shoes in the left display area.

Hint 60: On the right side of the first aisle in the movie and TV prop-storage area, the front of a yellow refrigerator sports a silver classic Mickey.

Hint 61: On the left side toward the end of the second aisle in the prop storage area, a framed photo of Mickey and Minnie sits inside a wire basket on top of a white bureau.

Hint 62: Inside the costuming building on the tram tour, you can spot a large Mickey clock on the far wall of the first sewing room to your left.

Hint 63: Later on the ride, you can see a small classic Mickey image inside the "D" of "Disney World" on the side of Walt Disney's airplane. The Mickey image on the tail of the plane is decorative, not hidden.

Hint 64: After the tram ride, look for a mural on the right wall just inside the entrance to the AFI display rooms. Just to the left of the tallest building in the mural, in the right center, is a Mickey Mouse statue on a tombstone. Atop the fourth building from the left side of the mural is Mickey's side-profile silhouette. On the right side of the fifth building from the left is a white side profile of his face.

### -Studio Catering Co.

Hint 65: At the side of the restaurant, a red classic Mickey lies on a black tile under a fire alarm on the right wall of the High Octane Refreshments Bar.

### -Walt Disney: One Man's Dream

Hint 66: On the left side of the display aisle (and before you are ushered into the theater), you see Walt Disney standing with a pointer in front of a wall map. On a desk to Walt's left, a coffee mug near a telephone has Donald Duck on it.

Hint 67: You can spot a green classic Mickey in the same scene. He's on the wall to the left of Walt.

### -Disney Junior – Live on Stage!

Hint 68: Classic Mickeys appear at times in the lighting and stage effects as well as on various stage props during the live show.

HINTS HINTS HINTS HINTS HINTS HINTS HINTS HINTS HINTS HINTS HINTS

### -The Hollywood Brown Derby restaurant

Hint 69: Classic Mickeys are in the clouds on the mural on the outside wall above the restaurant. One is at the far upper right of the mural, and another is at the far mid-left of the mural, above the "Stage 5" sign.

Hint 70: On a wall to the left in the waiting area, in the second row of pictures, you'll find a caricature of Jimmy Dodd (with his Mouse ears) from the 1950s' *Mickey Mouse Club* TV show.

### -The American Idol Experience

Hint 71: A classic Mickey image is on the lower light brown arch in the stage backdrop, between the second and third round archway lights (counting from the lower right of the arch). Another small, faint classic Mickey image is near the top of the same arch, between the fifth and sixth round archway lights (counting from the lower left of the arch).

Hint 72: In a video toward the end of the show, female singer Jordan Sparks is wearing a necklace with classic Mickey-shaped gems.

### -Sunset Boulevard

Hint 73: Midway down Sunset Boulevard toward the *Tower of Terror*, the outside scrollwork about halfway to the top of a blue building on the right side of the street has an upside-down classic Mickey in its design.

Hint 74: On the rear wall of Rosie's All-American Café, two regulators form classic Mickeys above the coffee and hot cocoa machines.

### -Beauty and the Beast

Hint 75: A classic Mickey is on a wind-up device on Cogsworth's back. The device has two holes for the "ears" and a larger circle for the "head." Sometimes this image is upside down.

### -Hollywood & Vine restaurant

Hint 76: Outside the restaurant, a silhouette of Roger Rabbit is in a window above and to the left of the entrance.

Hint 77: On the left wall inside, the "San Fernando Valley" wall mural has a stick figure Mickey on the far right, behind a pole.

Hint 78: Bushes form several classic Mickeys to the immediate left of the stick figure Mickey and also above him.

### -50's Prime Time Café

Hint 79: In the waiting area, washers shaped like classic Mickeys secure the white tabletops.

### -Near Indiana Jones
### Epic Stunt Spectacular!

Hint 80: There is a security booth (not an actual one) labeled "Gate 2." A full-body Mickey Mouse, along with other characters, is on a coffee mug inside the booth, and Mickey is also drawn at the upper left of a mail-tracking sheet. (Note: these images change from time to time.)

Hint 81: Several full-body two-dimensional Mickeys are on the bulletin boards inside the Backlot Express restaurant. One bulletin board is near the exit door facing *Star Tours*. A second is close by at the side of the seating area across from the mural of the city park.

### -Radio Disney sign

Hint 82: The "o" in the Radio Disney sign has a classic Mickey in the center.

### -Sci-Fi Dine-In Theater Restaurant

Hint 83: In the waiting area on the left wall as you enter is a poster for the movie *Attack of the 50 Ft. Woman*. A classic Mickey is behind her right knee, just off the highway.

Hint 84: Mickey Mouse in a graduation outfit is on an "Educational Reimbursement Program" notice on the lower middle of a bulletin board on a wall in the waiting area.

Hint 85: Face the kitchen, then look to the right of it at the tall fence in the right rear mural. You'll find Mickey's ears in the part of the mural that's above the right section of the fence. Look at the treetops. The Hidden Mickey is part of the outline of the center-right top of a tree that is located to the right of a tall palm tree.

Hint 86: Above the right corner of the tallest fence to the right of the kitchen, a bush Mickey along the top of the trees is waving with his left hand.

Hint 87: In the multicolored tiles above the kitchen door entrance (on the right as you face the kitchen) is a side profile of Mickey. He is outlined in yellow tiles and appears to be looking to his left (our right). Look first for his jaw, a curving line of yellow tiles in the middle of the mosaic square.

Hint 88: Watch the movie reel for Donald Duck, Mickey Mouse, and Tinker Bell. Donald is in a cartoon segment about a secretary who is kidnapped to another planet; Donald is one of the characters who chases her. The segment follows a clip of Walt Disney. Mickey appears later in the reel, in a "News of the Future" segment; he wears a spacesuit and waves to the crowd. Tinker Bell flies around above the word "Tomorrowland."

Hint 89: Stay alert for a youngster in a spacesuit during the movie reel, when the words "Calling All Boys! All Girls!" appear on the screen. A classic Mickey formed by a circle and two knobs is on the upper chest of the spacesuit, just below the helmet.

Hint 90: Silver classic Mickeys are at the sides of the car seats, on the running boards.

### -The Writer's Stop

Hint 91: Some of the theater lights hanging from the ceiling sport yellow classic Mickeys.

### -Pizza Planet Arcade

Hint 92: A classic Mickey is one of the constellations of stars above the counter registers. Focus on the left side of the rear wall, between Woody and the "Disney's Toy Story" sign.

Hint 93: A small, bright classic-Mickey star cluster appears above the counter registers on the right side of the rear wall. Look near the pizza-slice constellation.

Hint 94: Above the arcade games, in the moon near the top of the wall mural, you can spot a three-quarter Mickey profile facing left.

### -Stage 1 Company Store

Hint 95: A blue bird is stuck high on a side door of one of the tall merchandise cabinets inside the store. Classic Mickeys decorate the ends of a red scarf that is draped over the bird.

Hint 96: Look for an old bureau that's loaded with hats for sale and has paint cans at the very top. You'll find a green, painted classic Mickey near the center of the desktop.

Hint 97: In the middle of the store, across from the green-paint Hidden Mickey on the bureau, circles in the middle of a cloud at the upper left of a mural with a rainbow form an approximate classic Mickey.

Hint 98: Mickey Mouse's shorts (red with white buttons) are hanging on a line near one of the exit doors.

### -Mama Melrose's Ristorante Italiano

Hint 99: Just inside the entrance to the right, the Dalmatian has a black classic Mickey spot on its right shoulder (your left).

Hint 100: The right wall between the waiting room and the dining area bears a slightly distorted classic Mickey in the plaster. It's in the upper right corner, near the entrance door.

Hint 101: To the right of the check-in podium (as you face it), a green classic Mickey leaf is about one and a half feet above the bottom of the window, along the left edge.

Hint 102: The left wall between the waiting room and the dining area has a smaller classic Mickey plastered on the brick. You'll find it in the middle left part of the wall, just above the counter.

### -The Cars Meet and Greet area

Hint 103: The wing nut on Mater's engine air filter has Mickey ears.

Hint 104: A side profile of Mickey Mouse is etched in the lower part of a side wall to the left of the large brick wall mural that says "Radiator Springs, A Happy Place."

### -Streets of America

Hint 105: Some of the newspapers in a newsstand in the left lower area of a mural at the end of San Francisco Street feature articles about Steamboat Willie.

Hint 106: In the lower right and left sides of the same mural, some papers in a small newspaper dispenser feature articles about a recent Disney movie (at presstime, the movie was *Up*).

Hint 107: Along San Francisco Street, you'll find a Dalmatian on an address plaque on the wall above a barber pole. Three black spots above its front leg form a slightly distorted classic Mickey.

Hint 108: A watch with Mickey on its face is in the window of Sal's Pawn Shop, near the passage to *"Honey, I Shrunk the Kids" Movie Set Adventure.*

Hint 109: On the upper left wall of the second window (on the left as you face Venture Travel Service) is a picture of Walt Disney holding a Mickey Mouse doll in his right hand.

Hint 110: The same window holds three other Hidden Characters: classic Mickey holes decorate the lower edge of a lampshade and, in a photo propped on the desk below the shade, Mickey and Minnie are sitting on a bench looking out to a cruise ship at sea. We see just the backs of their heads.

Hint 111: A classic Mickey sand trap is in the left-most window as you face the New York backdrop at the end of the Streets of America.

### -End of Commissary Lane

Hint 112: Mickey Mouse, along with other characters, is on a coffee mug inside the faux security booth labeled "Gate 1." (Note: this mug changes from time to time.)

### -Animation Courtyard

Hint 113: Donald Duck and Goofy are etched on the ornamental arches that are adjacent to Animation Courtyard's main entrance arch.

### -The Magic of Disney Animation

Hint 114: The stage set in front of the seating area for the first part of *The Magic of Disney Animation* tour usually features a number of Hidden Mickeys. Check the large animator's desk for them. A coffee mug on the right side of the desk's middle shelf has a blue classic Mickey on it. Additional blue classic Mickeys can be found on the top of the desk. You can spot them at both the top of a pencil that's sticking out of a container and on the head of a standing figurine to the right. You can also see classic Mickey balloons on a large round button. It's at the top left of the animator's drawing board on the front of the desk.

Hint 115: In the movie during the first part of *The Magic of Disney Animation* tour, a man holds a coffee mug covered with classic Mickeys.

Hint 116: The carpet design inside the walking, self-guided part of the attraction usually includes classic Mickeys in the circles.

Hint 117: In the Character Greeting areas, you'll find Hidden Mickeys in three places. Classic Mickeys are in the background mural of the Sorcerer Mickey set. In the Lotso Bear greeting area, a classic Mickey is traced on a wood block, which is at the bottom of a stack of blocks on the left side of the greeting area. And on the left rear wall of Lotso's queue area, a light blue Sorcerer Mickey hat is in a painting. You'll find it on a bench in the left middle of the painting.

### -Toward Hollywood Blvd.

Hint 118: On the plaza, in front of Mickey's huge Sorcerer's Hat, a full-face Mickey Mouse formed by lights can often be spotted in the afternoon and evening.

### -Intersection of Hollywood & Sunset Blvds.

Hint 119: On both sides of Sunset Boulevard near its intersection with Hollywood Boulevard, you'll find small impressions in the cement sidewalks, near the curb. They read, "Mortimer & Co, 1928, Contractors." Mortimer Mouse was Mickey Mouse's first (and soon discarded) name; 1928 was the year he was "born."

### -Keystone Clothiers

Hint 120: Outside and above the shop, a Kodak billboard shows a girl bending forward, partially covering Mickey Mouse's handprints impressed in cement.

Hint 121: At Peevy's Polar Pipeline drink service, behind Keystone Clothiers, gauges or regulators form a classic Mickey, especially when viewed from behind.

### -Disney & Company

Hint 122: In an outside display window of the store, you'll find a sideways classic Mickey formed by metal circles on the side of a merchandise stand.

### -Mickey's of Hollywood

Hint 123: Classic Mickey holes are drilled in some of the store's metal support poles.

Hint 124: The caps on the ends of some merchandise racks are shaped like classic Mickeys.

Hint 125: In the Sorcerer section of the store, near a door to the street, you'll find cabinets with classic Mickey shapes on them.

Hint 126: "MICKEYS" is spelled out on four vertical dividers (two on each side of the store) that separate the sections of the store.

### -Cover Story

Hint 127: You'll find a design containing classic Mickeys on the outside of the store, next to The Darkroom. Look below the second-floor windows.

### -Near the charter bus area

Hint 128: Outside the park, near the charter bus area, a classic Mickey is stamped in cement. It's about nine or so benches (and three light poles) from the main entrance promenade as you head toward the walkway to the BoardWalk Resort. Look across from the "CG" marker on the cement.

### -Fantasmic!

Hint 129: When animated characters float up in large bubbles on the water screen, watch for Pinocchio. His bubble forms the head of a classic Hidden Mickey. Two bubbles beside it form the ears.

# Notes

# Disney's Animal Kingdom Scavenger Hunt

•  •  •  •  •  •  •  •  •  •  •  •  •  •  •  •  •  •  •  •  •  •  •  •  •  •  •

Clue 1: Watch the park's opening show and spot a net classic Mickey.
2 points

★ Your next stop is **Expedition Everest** in Asia. Walk through the Oasis, turn right in Discovery Island, and follow the path to Asia. One of the queue Hidden Mickeys is only in the FASTPASS and Single Rider queues. The rest are in the regular queue, which Disney calls the Standby line because you just walk into it and stand by for the attraction. So get a FASTPASS to use later and then join the Standby queue to search for the Mickeys in Clues 2 through 11 and Clue 13. Search for Clue 12 when you come back to take the ride at your FASTPASS time.

Clue 2: In the Standby line, search for a classic Mickey in the first sunken courtyard.
3 points

Clue 3: Look around for cloud Hidden Mickeys in a mural.
4 points for spotting two

Clue 4: Keep alert for pipes on a shelf that form a classic Mickey.
3 points

Clue 5: Look for a Hidden Mickey made of light-switch devices in a display.
3 points

Clue 6: Stay alert for Mickey on a book.
4 points

Clue 7: Search for Mickey on a handrail.
5 points

★ Visit **DINOSAUR** next. Go back through Discovery Island and then follow the walkway into DinoLand U.S.A. Find Hidden Mickeys on paintings just inside the *DINOSAUR* building.

Clue 21: Can you spot the Mickey on a tree trunk?
4 points

Clue 22: Now look for Mickey ears above a dinosaur.
3 points

Clue 23: After the ride begins, be alert for a Hidden Mickey on a greaseboard.
4 points

Clue 24: Find a classic Mickey on the red dinosaur in the mural behind the counter in the ride's photo-purchase area.
4 points

★ Walk into the queue for **It's Tough to be a Bug!** on Discovery Island.

Clue 25: When you get inside *The Tree of Life*, look for Mickey above the handicapped entrance doors.
4 points

★ Go to **Kali River Rapids** in Asia and find a classic Mickey formed by plates on the wall of one of the rooms you pass through on your way to the ride.

Clue 26: You're getting close when you see stone statues in the grass.
2 points

★ Stroll over to the **Maharajah Jungle Trek**. At the tiger exhibit area, find seven classic Hidden Mickeys in the building with arches.

Clue 27: Check in the water in the painting to the right of the first arch.
2 points

Clue 28: Look for the earring Mickey on the left mural inside the first arch.
2 points

Clue 29: Find a leaf Mickey on the left mural inside the first arch.
2 points

Clue 30: Search the right mural inside the first arch for a Hidden Mickey on a man.
2 points

Clue 31: Inside the building with arches, on the right wall, check the flowers on two square panels to find classic Mickeys.
2 points for one or more

Clue 32: Look for a classic Mickey in the mountains inside the second arch.
2 points

Clue 33: Now find a classic Mickey in the cloud formation inside the same arch.
2 points

Clue 34: After you exit the temple ruins, search for two Hidden Mickeys in the leaves to your left.
8 points for both

Clue 35: Scan the huge mural on the left outdoor wall at the Elds Deer Exhibit for a waving Hidden Mickey in orange flowers.
5 points

Clue 36: Further along the trail, before you get to the aviary entrance, try to spot a classic Mickey in a man's necklace in the carving on the wall.
2 points

★ Before or after an early lunch, wander over to the **Pangani Forest Exploration Trail** in Africa. Look for two Hidden Mickeys in the building with the Naked Mole Rat exhibit.

Clue 37: Find Mickey on a small box.
4 points

Clue 38: Spot a backpack with a Mickey emblem.
3 points

Clue 39: Past the gorilla viewing area, search for a Hidden Jafar.
5 points

★ Eat an early lunch to avoid the crowds. The Rainforest Café at the park entrance is a good place to eat and has an interesting ambiance. Tusker House Restaurant in Africa serves salads and sandwiches.

★ Consult the Times Guide and pick the next convenient shows of *Finding Nemo – The Musical* and *Festival of the Lion King*.

★ See **Finding Nemo – The Musical** at Theater in the Wild in DinoLand.

Clue 40: Look around for a Hidden Mickey near the stage.
3 points

Clue 41: Find two Hidden Mickeys in the show time signs outside.
4 points for spotting both

★ See **Festival of the Lion King** in Camp Minnie-Mickey.

Clue 42: Be alert for a classic Mickey on Timon the meerkat's float.
4 points

Clue 43: Now search for an upside-down classic Mickey on Timon's float.
4 points

Clue 44: Study the center stage for a classic Mickey.
4 points

(Tip: You can usually also find these Hidden Mickeys after the show has ended, while the crowd is exiting. If you need help, ask a Cast Member.)

★ Check other areas in **Camp Minnie-Mickey**.

**146**

Clue 45: Spot a rock classic Mickey in a wall near the *Greeting Trails*.
4 points

★ Now search the camp for a small cabin with classic Mickeys in the woodwork.

Clue 46: You'll find them on both the front and sides of the cabin.
2 points for spotting both

Clue 47: Search the ground near the creek outside the Lion King Theater for a rock classic Mickey.
4 points

Clue 48: Try to find a birdhouse with a Mickey Mouse cutout.
1 point

(Note: These birdhouses are moved around to different locations in Camp Minnie-Mickey periodically.)

Clue 49: Find Mickey Mouse's head on top of a nearby flagpole.
4 points

★ Go to Africa and take the *Wildlife Express Train* to Rafiki's Planet Watch to search **Conservation Station** for a Hidden Mickey bonanza.

Clue 50: Find the Hidden Mickey profile in the changing, repeating panels inside the entrance.
4 points

Clue 51: On the wall mural just to the right, spot a Mickey Mouse profile on an opossum.
4 points

Clue 52: Look for a butterfly wearing classic Mickeys.
3 points

Clue 53: Gaze closely at a spider nearby with a classic Mickey marking.
3 points

Clue 54: Spot a classic Mickey on an ostrich.
3 points

Clue 55: Look for a classic Mickey on a green snake.
3 points

**147**

Clue 56: Search for another classic Mickey on a lizard's ear.
4 points

Clue 57: Locate a side-profile Mickey on a hippo.
4 points

Clue 58: Glance at a llama for a classic Mickey.
3 points

Clue 59: A squirrel nearby shows off a classic Mickey.
3 points

Clue 60: Spot a classic Mickey on an alligator.
3 points

Clue 61: Find a frog with a tiny image of Mickey's face.
5 points

Clue 62: Scan a walrus for a Hidden Mickey.
4 points

Clue 63: Find the Hidden Mickey on an owl.
3 points

Clue 64: Search for the amazing Mickey image on a second butterfly!
5 points

Clue 65: Look up for a classic Mickey on a frog behind a monkey.
5 points

Clue 66: Scan the mural for a fish with a partially hidden classic Mickey.
5 points

Clue 67: Locate a butterfly with two Hidden Mickeys.
4 points

Clue 68: Look around carefully for a frog with a side-profile Mickey.
5 points

**148**

Clue 69: Find a yellow butterfly with a classic Mickey.
3 points

Clue 70: Look lower for a lizard with Mickey spots.
3 points

Clue 71: Scan overhead for a Mickey in tree leaves.
3 points

Clue 72: Next to the "Song of the Rainforest" area, spot a fly with a tiny classic Mickey on its back.
5 points

Clue 73: Search for a tiny flower Hidden Mickey at the first entrance to the "Song of the Rainforest" area.
4 points

Clue 74: Look for a classic Mickey indentation on a tree toward the front of the Rainforest area.
3 points

Clue 75: Don't stray far for a Mickey hole in a leaf.
4 points

Clue 76: Check the trees inside the Rainforest area for a side-profile Mickey shadow.
4 points

Clue 77: Look for the classic Mickey shadow on the ceiling near door number eight in the "Song of the Rainforest" area.
4 points

Clue 78: Now find a Hidden Mickey on a tree near door number six.
3 points

Clue 79: Search for a green moss side-profile Mickey in the Rainforest area.
4 points

Clue 80: Walk out to the front of the Rainforest area and search for a side-profile Mickey.
4 points

Clue 81: Spot a classic Mickey made of short plant stalks on the Grandmother Willow tree.
3 points

Clue 82: Also in the Rainforest area, spot a classic Mickey on a cockroach.
4 points

Clue 83: Now find a classic Mickey on a lizard on the same tree.
3 points

Clue 84: Look for a butterfly wearing a tiny Hidden Mickey on this tree.
5 points

Clue 85: Examine the grates around the bottoms of the trees in the main lobby.
2 points

Clue 86: Locate a Hidden Mickey on a plate in a window display at the rear of the lobby.
3 points

Clue 87: Spot a reptile classic Mickey on a ledge in the rear area displays and laboratories.
3 points

★ Walk outside to **Affection Section** to spot another classic Hidden Mickey.

Clue 88: Study the animals in the petting zoo.
4 points

(Note: These Hidden Mickeys come and go.)

★ Wander on over to the **Wildlife Express Train station** and look for classic Mickeys.

Clue 89: Examine the rafters inside the station.
2 points

★ Ride the train to Africa, then explore the area around **Harambe Fruit Market** to spot a large Mickey Mouse head in the cement.

Clue 90: Check the beginning of the cement and flag-

**150**

stone path at the side of the Fruit Market.
4 points

Clue 91: Turn left at the opposite end of the

path and follow the cement walkway a few feet to find a large, faint classic Mickey in the cement.
5 points

★ Outside the **Mombasa Marketplace store**, look for a classic Mickey formed by a small utility cover and the pebbles adjacent to it.

Clue 92: It's near an entrance door to the store.
5 points

★ Go to the far side of **Tamu Tamu Refreshments**.

Clue 93: Find another classic Mickey formed by a small utility cover and adjacent pebbles.
5 points

Clue 94: Marvel at a Hidden Baloo the bear inside the small seating area behind Tamu Tamu Refreshments.
5 points

Clue 95: Search for another Hidden Character here.
4 points

★ Walk a short way down the **path to Asia**.

Clue 96: Look over to *The Tree of Life* and spot the Hidden Mickey on it. (Psst! It's near the hippo.)
4 points

★ Cross the bridge to Discovery Island and amble on into **Pizzafari restaurant** to find six Hidden Mickeys.

Clue 97: Spot Mickey in the room across from the food order counters.
3 points

Clue 98: In the first dining room to the left as you walk down the hall, search for a tiny orange classic Mickey.
5 points

Clue 99: In the Nocturnal Room (the dining room directly to the left of the food counters as you face the counters), study the firefly wings.
3 points

Clue 100: In the Nocturnal Room, look around for a classic Mickey in the trees.
4 points

Clue 101: In the large room past the Nocturnal Room, find some spots on the wall in the tree branches.
3 points

Clue 102: Study an animal near these tree branches for a classic Mickey.
2 points

★ Return to DinoLand U.S.A. Enter **The Boneyard** and find four classic Mickeys.

Clue 103: Look under the drinking fountains inside the entrance.
3 points

Clue 104: On the lower level, locate a classic Mickey on a fence.
4 points

Clue 105: Walk upstairs. Go to the rear and observe the small classic Mickey in an archeology display.
2 points

Clue 106: Look around the children's dig area for Hidden Mickey hard hats.
2 points

★ Walk to the **Cretaceous Trail** in the middle of DinoLand and go dino hunting.

Clue 107: Find a dark Mickey on a dinosaur's back.
3 points

★ Go to **TriceraTop Spin**.

Clue 108: Search in front of the attraction for a classic Mickey on a dinosaur with a ball.
3 points

Clue 109: Spot a classic Mickey in one of the parking spaces near the attraction.
3 points

Clue 110: Study the nearby horned dinosaur studded with gems and find a Mickey pin.
4 points

Clue 111: Look around for Mickey on a blue dinosaur.
5 points

★ Check inside **Chester & Hester's Dinosaur Treasures** shop.

Clue 112: Study a big dinosaur for two Mickeys.
3 points for both

Clue 113: Now find a marionette Mickey in the shop.
2 points

★ Cross back to **Primeval Whirl** and look for classic Mickeys on the outside of the attraction.

Clue 114: Check the meteors.
5 points for two or more

Clue 115: Watch the parade (usually scheduled for 4:00 p.m.) for classic Mickey headlights and a classic Mickey antenna.
3 points for spotting both

★ Walk to the **Creature Comforts shop on Discovery Island** between Pizzafari restaurant and the bridge to Africa.

Clue 116: Search inside Creature Comforts for black classic Mickeys on an animal.
5 points for both

★ Enter the **Island Mercantile** shop.

Clue 117: Spot a classic Mickey on a wall.
5 points

★ Back outside **on Discovery Island**, find a classic Mickey made of green moss.

Clue 118: Study the front of The Tree of Life.
5 points

★ Stroll to the **Flame Tree Barbecue Restaurant** to find two classic Mickeys.

Clue 119: Search the ground in the food order area for a rock classic Mickey.
4 points

Clue 120: Spot a classic Mickey in the seating area outside.
2 points

★ Go to the **Rainforest Café entrance sign** inside the park.

Clue 121: Look for a Hidden Mickey on the sign.
3 points

★ Keep your eyes open **as you leave the park**.

Clue 122: Search the outside walls of the ticket booths for Hidden Mickeys.
4 points for two

Clue 123: Outside the entrance turnstiles, check the metal grates around some of the trees near the tram loading area.
2 points

Now tally your score.

**Total Points for Disney's Animal Kingdom =**

**How'd you do?**

Up to 176 points – Bronze
177 - 350 points – Silver
351 points and over – Gold
439 points - Perfect Score

You may have done even better if you earned bonus points in *Expedition Everest*.

**Caution:
Don't peek at this
section unless you
really want help!**

### -Park Opening Show

Hint 1: A blue classic Mickey-shaped net is on the side (usually the left) of the characters' safari vehicle.

## Asia

### -Expedition Everest

(Note: Hints 2 through 11 and 13 apply to Hidden Mickeys you'll find in the Standby queue. Hints 11 and 13 are for Mickeys that can be spotted in both the Standby and FASTPASS queues, while Hint 12 is a Hidden Mickey that you'll only find in the FASTPASS and Single Rider queues.)

Hint 2: The base of a Yeti statue in a sunken courtyard past the first room (an office) has a classic Mickey made of a central circle with swirls for ears.

Hint 3: Just past the first room, classic Mickeys are in the clouds on the left and right sides of a Yeti mural on a wall of a red building.

Hint 4: As you enter the second building, an upside-down classic Mickey is formed by the highest pipes on the top shelf in the right corner.

Hint 5: In Tashi's Trek and Tongba Shop, light-switch devices in a glass case on the left side of the queue form a classic Mickey.

Hint 6: Inside the Yeti Museum, on the right side of the queue after the first left turn, look for a Yeti book at the far left of the book display. A partial image of Mickey's head and ears is imprinted in the snow on the book's front cover.

Hint 7: Just past the snow Mickey, a classic Mickey is etched into the top of a wooden handrail.

Hint 8: Also in the Yeti Museum, dents in a kettle in the second display form a classic Mickey.

Hint 9: The museum also offers a classic Mickey in an "animal track." It's at the lower left of a tall glass cabinet display labeled "Documenting Bio-Diversity." Look near the top of the third paper from the left, above the label "Small Mammal Tracks."

Hint 10: The next to last display cabinet in the museum has a photo of a bear with ears that look like Mickey's ears. The bear is on the right side of the cabinet, under the words "The Yeti, Interpreting the Findings."

Hint 11: In the last room before boarding, look for a photo of a woman in blue listening to a hand-held radio. Mickey in his Sorcerer's Hat is etched on a wall to the woman's left.

Hint 12: In the Yeti Museum, a sideways classic Mickey is formed by three dents in a lantern in the second display. You can spot this lantern image from both the FASTPASS and Single Rider queues.

Hint 13: In the loading area, look for a classic Mickey in the blue scrollwork above the first window outside.

Hint 14: In the first part of the ride, as your train is climbing the mountain, a dark, melted classic Mickey-shaped spot appears in the snow to your left. The "ear" farthest away from the train is contiguous with a larger dark spot above it.

Bonus Points Hint: The ride photos from various WDW attractions often include Hidden Mickeys. Check the photos on the monitors at the unloading area. A small white classic Hidden Mickey might be present on the ground to the left of the ride vehicle.

Hint 15: Small gold balls form classic Mickeys at the bottom of both sides of a merchandise display in the middle of the gift shop at the ride exit. The display is across from the photo pickup area.

Hint 16: In a merchandise cabinet in the middle of the gift shop, a brown chest is on the right side of an upper shelf. The shelf faces the exit door to the left (as you exit the ride). Three circles near the right front of the chest form a classic Mickey that tilts to the right.

Hint 17: Outside and across from the Serka Zong Bazaar shop, an upside-down classic Mickey is etched near the top of the second stone tablet from the edge closest to the shop.

Hint 18: Outside the attraction, base camp supplies hang in the Gupta's Gear area. A three-circle image hangs among these supplies, near the second post from the end nearest the restrooms.

# Africa

### -Kilimanjaro Safaris

Hint 19: In elephant country, and about halfway through the ride, the island in the flamingo pond is shaped like a classic Hidden Mickey. It's to the left of your ride vehicle.

Hint 20: The rocks in the lion area are arranged to resemble Donald Duck. Spot his cap first, then his face, eyes, and beak.

# DinoLand U.S.A.

### -DINOSAUR

Hint 21: Just inside the building entrance, on the right side of the queue, look at the tree at the far left of the painting. There's a classic Mickey on the tree trunk; it's across from a lower right branch.

Hint 22: In a painting on the wall you face before you take the first right turn in the entrance queue, you can spot classic Mickey ears along the left side of the red-dish explosion cloud above the middle dinosaur.

Hint 23: Just as the ride starts and before you travel back in time, a classic Mickey at the lower left corner of a white greaseboard appears to the left of your vehicle.

Hint 24: On the mural behind the counter in the ride's photo-purchase area, a large red dinosaur has a small classic Mickey on its lower neck.

## Discovery Island

### -It's Tough to be a Bug!

Hint 25: Inside *The Tree of Life*, look for the handi-capped entrance doors to *It's Tough to be a Bug!* (You reach them before you get to the main entrance doors to the theater.) Look at the upper left area near the doors to find a small dark classic Mickey.

## Asia

### -Kali River Rapids

Hint 26: Along the entrance queue, keep your eyes peeled for stone statues in the grass. As you enter the next room, look at the lower left corner of the wall. Three of the plates on the wall above the bicycle form a classic Mickey, tilted down to the right. (Note: these images change from time to time.)

### -Maharajah Jungle Trek

Hint 27: To the right of the first arch, swirls in the water under a tiger form a classic Mickey.

Hint 28: Inside the first arch, on the left mural, the king's gold earring forms an upside-down classic Mickey.

Hint 29: Inside the first arch, on the left mural, three leaves under the wrist of the king's extended arm form a classic Mickey.

Hint 30: Inside the first arch, on the right mural, a man is wearing an upside-down classic Mickey gold earring.

Hint 31: On the right wall inside the building with arches, two square panels are decorated with flowers. Some of the outer flowers have circles at the bases of their petals that form classic Mickeys.

Hint 32: Inside the second arch, on the left mural, there's a small classic Mickey in a brown rock formation on the left side of the mountains.

Hint 33: Inside the second arch, on the right mural, a classic Mickey appears in the upper part of the left cloud formation.

Hint 34: As you exit the temple ruins, turn to your immediate left to a large wall mural. Among the leaves is a dark green classic Mickey. It's about nine feet above the ground and one foot from the bricks at the left side of the mural. Another even darker green classic Mickey is further to the right on this wall mural. It's above the tiger running to the left, and between two large, light-green fan-shaped leaves.

Hint 35: In the Elds Deer Exhibit, look left to the huge outdoor wall mural. Mickey is hiding in the right center of the mural, below the third (from the left) of four vertical brick cracks, in some orange flowers and green leaves.

Hint 36: On a wall to the right, just before you reach the aviary entrance, you'll find an upside-down classic Mickey in the necklace of a man in the middle carving.

# Africa

### -Pangani Forest Exploration Trail

Hint 37: To the left of the entrance to the building with the Naked Mole Rat Exhibit, a small box of Asepso soap on a shelf behind the desk lamp has a classic Mickey as the "o" in Asepso. You may need to crouch down to spot it.

Hint 38: In the far left corner of the room with the Naked Mole Rat Exhibit, a backpack sports a small classic Mickey emblem on the left side.

Hint 39: A three-dimensional head of Jafar is carved out of a 25- to 30-foot rock. You'll find it past the gorilla viewing area, to the right of the first section of the first suspension bridge.

# DinoLand U.S.A.

### -Finding Nemo – The Musical

Hint 40: Three bubbles touch to form a classic Mickey at the lower left of the stage.

Hint 41: Two sideways classic Mickeys formed by bubbles are in the outdoor signs announcing the show times for the day. One is in the bottom right corner of the signs, and another is under the 1:00 time disk. These signs are posted on the walkway from Asia and on the walkway from the rest of DinoLand U.S.A.

# Camp Minnie-Mickey

### -Festival of the Lion King

Hint 42: A white classic Mickey is painted on the lower middle front of Timon's (and the giraffe's) float. You can see it as the float enters the arena.

**160**

Hint 43: An upside-down white classic Mickey is on the lower right side of Timon's float, under the giraffe's front leg.

Hint 44: A classic Mickey in relief is on the lower side of the center stage, to the right of some steps. It is often facing the Elephant section of the audience.

### – Near the last Greeting Trail

Hint 45: A rock classic Mickey is directly across from the entrance to the last *Greeting Trail*, at the upper part of a short rock wall. One "ear" is light purple.

### -Cabin on the grounds

Hint 46: Across from the entrance to *Festival of the Lion King*, a cabin housing an ice cream shop has classic Mickeys in the woodwork along the front and sides.

Hint 47: A classic Mickey made of rocks is next to the creek between the Lion King Theater and the small food cabin. It's near the second fence section and between the creek and the food cabin, close to Donald Duck.

Hint 48: A birdhouse is often hanging from the front of Chip 'n' Dale's Cookie Cabin. It has a side-profile cutout of Mickey Mouse. Other such birdhouses may be found elsewhere in Camp Minnie-Mickey.

Hint 49: Mickey Mouse's head is on top of the flagpole by the water well, opposite the entrance to the outdoor theater (and before you get to the second bridge to Camp Minnie-Mickey).

# Rafiki's Planet Watch

### -Conservation Station

Hint 50: The front wall inside the entrance has a section of changing, repeating panels. A small side profile of Mickey Mouse is in the center of the orange starfish.

Hint 51: Find an opossum on the right side of the mural just inside the entrance. There is a side profile of Mickey Mouse in its eye.

Hint 52: Above the opossum, at the upper right, a butterfly has classic Mickeys on its wings.

Hint 53: About six feet up from the floor, not far from the opossum, a spider has a light pink classic Mickey marking on its thorax.

Hint 54: On the wall to the left of the restrooms, near the entrance, the pupil of an ostrich's eye is a classic Mickey.

Hint 55: Toward the middle of the mural at the front, near the entrance, a green snake sports a black classic Mickey on its upper back.

Hint 56: Near the upper right border of the changing screen, a dark classic Mickey marking is at the top of a green lizard's ear, above a deer.

Hint 57: A hippopotamus is the fifth animal from the left at the bottom of the entrance mural on the left wall. A side-profile Mickey is on its lower jaw, under the middle tooth.

Hint 58: To the immediate left of the hippopotamus, a llama sports a dark brown classic Mickey on its neck.

Hint 59: Under the hippopotamus, a squirrel has a black classic Mickey pupil.

Hint 60: On the hippo's right side, an alligator has a small dark classic Mickey to the left of its green eye.

Hint 61: To the right of the alligator, Mickey Mouse's smiling face is under a frog's right eye.

Hint 62: Directly above the frog with the smiling Mickey is a walrus with a dark classic Mickey on the left side (your right) of his neck.

**162** Hint 63: A bit farther along on this left wall mural, the pupils of an owl's eyes are classic Mickeys.

Hint 64: The entrance murals curve toward the inside of the building. On the right curving mural, look closely for the butterfly with an image of Mickey's face on its body (not on its wings!).

Hint 65: Midway along the right curving mural, high up near the ceiling, a classic Mickey-shaped marking is on the tan skin under the middle of the frog's face. The frog is behind a red-faced monkey.

Hint 66: Toward the top and near the end of the left side of the entrance mural, a dark classic Mickey, partially hidden by an octopus nearby, is on the side of a fish, to the left of the fish's fin.

Hint 67: Along the bottom of the right mural as you near Rafiki's Theater, two black classic Mickeys are near the bottom of the wings of an orange butterfly under a monkey.

Hint 68: Near the bottom of the same mural, just before the theater, a side-profile Mickey is in a silver frog's left pupil.

Hint 69: Before the first entrance to the "Song of the Rainforest" area, about halfway up the wall and above a bat, a yellow butterfly has a black classic Mickey on its left wing.

Hint 70: In the same area, a tan and green lizard has a group of spots directly behind the eye that form an upside-down classic Mickey.

Hint 71: A hole in the tree leaves overhead resembles a classic Mickey. It's directly above the first entrance.

Hint 72: The fly with a tiny classic Mickey on its back is on the left panel of the first entrance to the "Song of the Rainforest" area.

Hint 73: On the same panel, a tiny yellow flower classic Mickey blooms on a green plant near the floor.

Hint 74: Turn to the right panel at the same entrance to the Rainforest area to see a classic Mickey indentation on a tree. It's about four feet up from the floor.

Hint 75: Look for a classic Mickey hole in a green leaf near the Mickey indentation in Hint 74.

Hint 76: Now go inside to see a side-profile Mickey shadow about seven feet up from the floor on the front of a tree inside the Rainforest area.

Hint 77: Above and in front of door number eight in the Rainforest area, you can spot a dark classic Mickey shadow on the ceiling to the right.

Hint 78: A white classic Mickey is outlined on a tree by door number six, to the left of the words "The Accidental Florist."

Hint 79: Turn around and walk out toward the lobby to look at the right side of the tree with "The Song of the Rainforest" sign (the Grandmother Willow tree). A rear horizontal panel has a green moss side-profile Mickey about six feet up from the floor.

Hint 80: A side-profile Mickey indentation appears on the same tree under the sign and to the lower right (as you face her) of Grandmother Willow's face. (Tip: You have to walk further into the lobby to spot it.)

Hint 81: Three plant stalks form a classic Mickey in the mural near the floor on the bottom left of the Grandmother Willow tree (as you face it from the lobby).

Hint 82: To the right of the Grandmother Willow tree, there is a cockroach display inside a tree in front of the "Song of the Rainforest" area. A cockroach inside and toward the back of the tree bears a dark classic Mickey on its back.

Hint 83: A lizard above the "Giant Cockroach" sign on the same tree has a classic Mickey above its front leg.

Hint 84: On the left front of the tree with the cockroach display, a light brown butterfly about six and a half feet up from the floor has a tiny black classic Mickey on its

back between the wings.

Hint 85: The grates around the bottoms of the trees in the lobby have classic Mickey patterns, as do those outside by *Affection Section*.

Hint 86: A classic Mickey on a "Microtiter Plate" is usually in the first display room to the right in the rear of the lobby. Look into the second window of the "Wildlife Tracking Center." The plate changes color as you watch it!

Hint 87: A classic Mickey made of three containers with reptile skins is on a ledge in the far left window of a room with reptiles.

### -Affection Section

Hint 88: One of the animals usually has a classic Mickey shaved into its coat.

### -Wildlife Express Train station

Hint 89: High up in the rafters inside the train station, look for classic Mickeys where the beams intersect.

# Africa

### -In and around Harambe

Hint 90: At one side of the Harambe Fruit Market, a short cement and flagstone path with benches leads through some trees. A large Mickey Mouse head in the cement marks the beginning of the path. It's several feet in diameter.

Hint 91: At the opposite end of this short path, turn left onto the cement walkway and walk a few feet. Nearby you'll find a faint depression in the cement that forms a very large classic Mickey (six feet or more in diameter). This HM is best seen after a rain when the pavement is wet. It is often partially covered with parked strollers.

Hint 92: Outside, near an entrance door to the Mombasa Marketplace store, you'll find a classic Mickey formed by a small utility cover (with the letter "D" in the middle) and the pebbles adjacent to it. The cover is on the path on the side facing the Tusker House Restaurant.

Hint 93: Near Tamu Tamu Refreshments, on the walkway that connects Africa and Asia, a small utility cover and the pebbles adjacent to it form a similar classic Mickey. Here, the utility cover has the letter "S" in the middle.

Hint 94: Inside the small seating area behind Tamu Tamu Refreshments, a white Hidden Baloo (the bear) is on the wall nearest the path to Asia. He's often covered by a curtain.

Hint 95: Inside the small seating area behind Tamu Tamu Refreshments, a Hidden Scar (the lion) is on a corner wall and under vases that are in recessed openings.

Hint 96: On the back of *The Tree of Life*, and visible from the path between Africa and Asia, is an upside-down classic Mickey. Look above the eye of the hippopotamus to spot him.

# Discovery Island

### -Pizzafari restaurant

Hint 97: A yellow classic Mickey image is under a bat, which is on a wall in the seating area across from the food order counters. As you enter the room, turn left to face the rear wall and look for the bat on the right.

Hint 98: On the rear wall of the first dining room to the left as you walk down the hall away from the food order area, a tiny orange classic Mickey is at the lower left of a turtle shell.

Hint 99: On the left rear wall of the Nocturnal Room (the dining room directly to the left of the food counters as you face the counters), the wings of the lower left firefly resemble Mickey Mouse ears.

**166**

Hint 100: In the same room, a classic Mickey made of tree leaves lies near a reddish raccoon. It's tilted with the "ears" to the left as you face the wall.

Hint 101: In the large room just past the Nocturnal Room, a gray spot with two white ears on the far wall forms a classic Mickey in the tree branches, to the right of the leopard.

Hint 102: On this same wall, a classic Mickey formed by black spots is directly behind the middle of the leopard's front leg.

# DinoLand U.S.A.

### -The Boneyard

Hint 103: Just inside the entrance, you'll find a reddish-brown classic Mickey pattern in the flooring under the drinking fountains.

Hint 104: On the lower level, to the left of the main entrance, look for a small, fenced-in area containing archeology supplies. A white hard hat hangs on the rear fence. On the front of the hat above the letter "B," blue swirls form an upside-down classic Mickey.

Hint 105: Upstairs to the rear left, in a fenced off archeology display, three coins on a table form a classic Mickey.

Hint 106: On the right side of the children's dig area, in a small display, a fan and two hard hats form a classic Mickey.

### -Cretaceous Trail

Hint 107: At one end of this short trail in the middle of Dinoland, you'll find a large dinosaur. Three dark spots on its middle back form a classic Mickey.

### -TriceraTop Spin

Hint 108: In front of *TriceraTop Spin*, a green dinosaur balances a red and yellow striped ball on its horns. A classic Mickey is formed in the scales on the dino's right side, under the front horn.

Hint 109: In the parking spaces across from *TriceraTop Spin,* a classic Mickey can be found in the cement at the front of the second parking space from the horned dinosaur.

Hint 110: On the right side of the horned dinosaur (as you face it), a gold "Steamboat Willie" Cast Member pin is located on a spine on the dinosaur's upper back, near a large silver medallion.

Hint 111: A dark blue classic Mickey is near the left wrist of the blue dinosaur holding the "Chester & Hester's Dino-Rama" sign near *TriceraTop Spin.*

### -Chester & Hester's Dinosaur Treasures shop

Hint 112: Inside Chester & Hester's shop, a large green dinosaur holds Mr. Potato Head, who is wearing a Mickey safari hat and is eating a Mickey ice cream bar.

Hint 113: Inside, in the middle of the shop, a Mickey Mouse marionette hangs high along the right side.

### -Primeval Whirl

Hint 114: In the outside decorations, the sides of several meteors sport classic Mickey craters. One is under "Head for the Hills," one is over the "Primeval Whirl" sign, and a third is on the right side of the attraction near a dinosaur holding a sign.

Hint 115: The parade (usually at 4:00 p.m.) abounds in classic and décor Mickeys. The first jeep has classic Mickey headlights and the last vehicle has classic Mickey antenna dishes on the flagpole.

## Discovery Island

### -Creature Comforts shop

Hint 116: Black classic Mickeys are on the backs of the large beetles that decorate

some of the store's merchandise stands. One is on the mid left of a beetle under a zebra. Another beetle on the lower part of a stand (usually found at the rear of the store) has a classic Mickey on each of its wings.

### -Island Mercantile Shop

Hint 117: A classic Mickey made of spots is on a lower cell of an orange and blue bumblebee honeycomb on an inside post. It's on the right rear wall opposite the entrance doors closest to the walkway to the Oasis.

### -The Tree of Life

Hint 118: On the front of *The Tree of Life*, facing the Oasis and about one-third the distance up the tree trunk from the bottom, is a classic Mickey made of green moss. You'll find it to the left of the buffalo.

### -Flame Tree Barbecue Restaurant

Hint 119: In the food order area, rocks embedded in the ground form a classic Mickey at the front edge of the rock border and next to the second post from the right wall.

Hint 120: At the outside seating area behind the food order counters, grates on the ground near trees have classic Mickey circles. Find them near the first set of tables to the right, where there is a statue of a frog holding up a pig. These grates can also be found in other nearby areas.

## Oasis

### -Rainforest Café

Hint 121: A green lizard at the Rainforest Café entrance sign that is inside the park has an upside-down classic Mickey in the middle of the circles on its neck.

## Outside the entrance turnstiles to the park

Hint 122: When you head out of the park, turn back as you pass the ticket booths. You'll find two rock classic Mickeys, one on the right-hand lower corner of the wall of the rightmost ticket booth and the other in the wall of the leftmost ticket booth near the ground and toward the front of the booth's left side.

Hint 123: Outside the entrance turnstiles, near the tram loading area, the metal grates at the bases of some of the trees incorporate classic Mickeys in their design.

# Resort Hotel Scavenger Hunt

• • • • • • • • • • • • • • • • • • • • • • •

Walt Disney World's resort hotels are filled with Mickeys, hidden and otherwise. The majority are what I like to call décor Hidden Mickeys, imaginative decorations that vary among the hotels and change periodically over time. Such Hidden Mickeys can be found along hotel hallways in the carpet, wallpaper, and lampshades. They appear in the guestrooms on covers for drinking glasses, bedspreads, pillows, day beds, furniture, lamps, lamp shades, room curtains, shower curtains, wall pictures, wallpaper, carpets, soap, the outer wrapping of toilet paper rolls, and other items. Guest laundry rooms sometimes have Hidden Mickeys on the soap vending machines and in the bubbles on wall paintings, and resort laundry bins and carts show off classic and side-profile Mickeys.

In the restaurants, pancakes, waffles, butter pats, pasta, pizza, pepperoni on the pizza, and the arrangement of dishes and condiments, among other items, are sometimes Mickey-shaped. Sample menu displays in food order areas often have food items arranged to form classic Mickeys. Mugs, paper plates, and other items in the gift shops can sport Mickeys. Even the utilities embrace Mickey. Manhole covers and survey markers throughout Walt Disney World often have classic Mickey designs in the center.

Generally, I do not include such décor Mickeys in the scavenger hunts unless they are truly unique (as many of the carpet Mickeys are) and are easily accessible to Hidden Mickey hunters at the hotels and other WDW areas. So don't be surprised to discover dozens of Mickeys at the hotels you visit that aren't included in this scavenger hunt. They're fun to spot but you don't get points for finding them.

The best way to hunt for Hidden Mickeys at the hotels is by car. However, buses to all the WDW hotels are available from

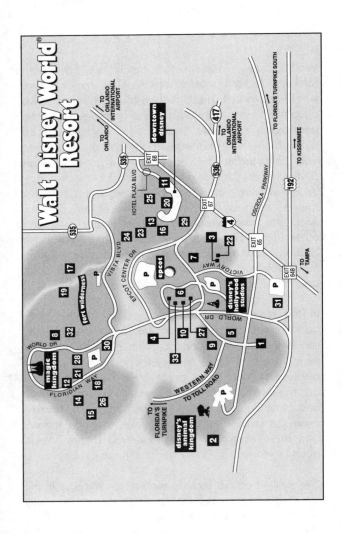

1 All-Star Resorts
2 Animal Kingdom Lodge
3 Art of Animation (opening summer 2012)
4 Beach Club
5 Blizzard Beach
6 BoardWalk
7 Caribbean Beach
8 Contemporary
9 Coronado Springs
10 Dolphin
11 Downtown Disney
12 Grand Floridian
13 Lake Buena Vista Golf Course
14 Magnolia Golf Course
15 Oak Trail Golf Course
16 Old Key West
17 Osprey Ridge Golf Course

18 Palm Golf Course
19 Pioneer Hall
20 Pleasure Island, in Downtown Disney
21 Polynesian
22 Pop Century
23 Port Orleans – French Quarter
24 Port Orleans – Riverside
25 Saratoga Springs
26 Shades of Green
27 Swan
28 Transportation and Ticket Center
29 Typhoon Lagoon
30 WDW Speedway
31 ESPN Wide World of Sports Complex
32 Wilderness Lodge
33 Yacht Club
P Parking

Downtown Disney (the major bus depot is at the far end of the Marketplace). If you choose to bus around, be prepared for leisurely hunting. You won't be able to visit as many hotels in a given time frame as you would with a car.

Of course, driving means parking, and it's not always a slam-dunk. Guard gates stand watch at most WDW hotels. When you drive up, tell the guard that you're a Hidden Mickey freak and want to look for Hidden Mickeys at the hotel. You'll generally be greeted with a smile, an opened gate, and a wave — along with a "Good luck!" or "Go freak out!" to encourage you on your quest. In the event you aren't allowed to park, drive on to another hotel on the scavenger hunt and take transportation (bus, boat or monorail) to the one you want to explore. If you're really lucky, you may have a spouse, friend or family member who is willing to drop you off and pick you up.

Again, be considerate of other guests and Cast Members. Ask permission to look around restaurants and avoid searching for Hidden Mickeys at meal times unless you are one of the diners. Even then be careful to stay out of the way — especially of waiters with full trays. Let others share in the fun by telling them what you are up to if they notice you looking around.

Two important notes:

• I've arranged this hunt in a logical, efficient progression that I imagine you could follow in a car. However, you may want to hunt just one hotel or group of sister hotels at a time. That's why I list the perfect score for each resort hotel (and hotel group) in parentheses after the hotel (or group) name in the Clues section.

• This scavenger hunt includes only those WDW resorts in which I found Hidden Mickeys. If I found no convincing (to me) Hidden Mickeys in a hotel, I didn't include it in the hunt. Keep your eyes open; you may spot a Hidden Mickey that I haven't found (yet).

During your Hidden Mickey hunt around WDW property, pay attention to the Disney buses. You may get lucky! The Disney Cruise Line bus has a Hidden Pluto on each side of the gold scrollwork on the front of the bus between the headlights. One or more general Disney transport buses sometimes sports a classic Mickey on the rear of the bus, usually related to rear upper or lower lights. If you spot one or more of these images, give yourself 5 bonus points for each one.

I'll start with Animal Kingdom Lodge Resort, but you can start (and stop) wherever you want. Have fun!

# Animal Kingdom Lodge Resort
# (107 points)

Clue 1: Look up for a classic Mickey outside near the hotel's main entrance.
2 points

Clue 2: Find a classic Mickey on a wall mural between the outer and inner entrance doors to the main lobby.
2 points

Clue 3: Inside the main lobby, spot a classic Mickey on a chandelier.
3 points

Clue 4: Check the logs banded to wood supports around the main lobby. Find any classic Mickeys?
2 points

Clue 5: Look for a classic Mickey on the rock formation next to the short bridge on the right side of the main lobby (as you face it on entering).
4 points

Clue 6: Search the Kudu Trail at the rear of the lobby for a classic Mickey on a post.
4 points

Clue 7: Try to spot a green Hidden Mickey in side profile outside the rear doors of the main lobby. He's on the vine-covered column, on your right as you exit, and he's looking into the lobby.
5 points

**175**

Clue 8: On the trail to Arusha Rock Overlook, outside the rear exit from the main

lobby, explore the decorative reliefs on the rock wall for a giraffe with a classic Mickey.
3 points

Clue 9: Spot another classic Mickey along the walkway in Arusha Rock Overlook.
4 points

Clue 10: Search for a classic Mickey on the rock wall as you descend the stairs from the right side of the main lobby to Boma restaurant.
4 points

Clue 11: Examine the chairs inside Boma restaurant.
2 points

Clue 12: Inside Jiko restaurant, check out the ceiling above the large oven exhausts.
2 points

Clue 13: From inside Jiko, spot a classic Mickey out the window.
5 points

Clue 14: From the path alongside the walkway to the pool's water slide, find a classic Mickey impression low on a rock.
4 points

Clue 15: Further along this walkway, around the back of the swimming pool, look for a light-colored classic Mickey cut into the rock wall.
4 points

Clue 16: From a fence at the flamingo overlook, study the rock wall for a classic Mickey.
4 points

★ Walk back to The Mara and then turn and walk toward the pool.

Clue 17: On your way, look down for a classic Mickey.
5 points

 Clue 18: Search the wall outside in the

back of The Mara eatery seating area for a classic Mickey.
4 points

★ Now find three classic Mickeys inside The Mara food area.

Clue 19: One is on the left upper wall.
3 points

Clue 20: Another is above the bakery.
3 points

Clue 21: The third is on the right upper wall.
3 points

★ *Inside the Lodge* (8 points)

Clue 22: Spot a classic Mickey in the elevator to the Fitness Center.
2 points

Clue 23: Walk around to spot some classic Mickeys in the carpet below the fifth floor as well as either on or above the fifth floor.
4 points for two or more

Clue 24: Search for Mickey near the main Zebra Trail on the third floor.
2 points

★ Walk to *Kidani Village*. (27 points)

Clue 25: Look for Mickey on a clock.
4 points

Clue 26: Search high for Mickey in the lobby.
5 points

Clue 27: Spot him as you approach Sanaa restaurant.
4 points

Clue 28: Locate Mickey on a wall inside Sanaa.
3 points

Clue 29: Study Sanaa's dining tables.
3 points

Clue 30: Now leave the restaurant and find Mickey on a rock outside.
4 points

Clue 31: Stroll the hallways for carpet Mickeys.
4 points for two or more

# Disney's All-Star Resorts
# (16 points)

### ★ *All-Star Sports Resort* (7 points)

Clue 32: Go to the main building gift shop and find classic Mickeys in the carpet.
2 points

Clue 33: Walk around the food court for a Hidden Mickey on the wall.
3 points

Clue 34: Find the classic Mickey in the cement outdoors behind and to the right of the registration building. (Psst! He's near the Mickey Mouse statue.)
2 points

### ★ *All-Star Music Resort* (5 points)

Clue 35: Examine the Jazz Inn courtyard to spot classic Mickey ears.
3 points

Clue 36: Take a look at the boots in the Country Fair area.
2 points

### ★ *All-Star Movies Resort* (4 points)

Clue 37: Find a classic Mickey in a display window of the gift shop.
3 points

Clue 38: Check out Andy's Room in the resort's "Toy Story" section.

1 point

# Coronado Springs Resort (38 points)

**Clue 39:** Take a good look at the large wooden doors at the front entrance to the main lobby.
3 points

**Clue 40:** Search for Mickey on the seating near the lobby fountain.
5 points

**Clue 41:** Don't miss a tiny Mickey as you enter the registration area.
4 points

**Clue 42:** Now study the wooden doors at the exit labeled El Centro.
3 points

**Clue 43:** Walk to the hallway outside the Veracruz Exhibit Hall in the Convention Center and look around for two classic Mickeys.
4 points for spotting both

**Clue 44:** Examine the cement near the Marina rental gazebo.
4 points

★ Around the *Dig Site* (15 points)

**Clue 45:** Spot a classic Mickey at the Dig Site swimming pool on a wall facing the lake.
3 points

**Clue 46:** Now find a classic Mickey on a wall facing the Dig Site pool.
3 points

**Clue 47:** Look for a whitish classic Mickey on a stone block on the Mayan pyramid at the Dig Site.
4 points

**Clue 48:** Spot Mickey near the Dig Site restrooms.
3 points

**Clue 49:** Check the bus stop signs around the periphery of the resort.
2 points for one or more

# Pop Century Resort (43 points)

Clue 50: Search for a fishbowl with a Hidden Mickey near the check-in area.
4 points

Clue 51: Find Mickey behind the registration counter.
4 points

Clue 52: Look low for Hidden Mickeys at the Everything Pop Food Court.
3 points for two or more

Clue 53: Locate Hidden Mickeys on walls in the food court.
4 points for four or more

Clue 54: In the gift shop adjoining the Everything Pop Food Court, find Hidden Mickeys on merchandise stands.
2 points

Clue 55: Also in the gift shop, search for two classic Mickeys on the wall.
4 points for both

Clue 56: Spot a classic Mickey on a wall near the Computer Pool.
4 points

Clue 57: Now look near the Computer Pool for two Hidden Mickeys that could help you type.
2 points for both

Clue 58: Marvel at a Hidden Mickey on a wall behind Mowgli on the '60s building.
5 points

Clue 59: Find Hidden Mickeys in laundry rooms near the Hippy Dippy Pool and the Bowling Pool.
4 points for four

Clue 60: Search for Mickey's name near the Bowling Pool (and, just for fun, a reference to "Disneyland" nearby).
4 points

Clue 61: Look around for a Hidden Mickey near the bus stop out front of the Pop Century lobby.
3 points

## Caribbean Beach Resort (23 points)

Clue 62: Say hello to Mickey outside the main entrance to Old Port Royale!
3 points

Clue 63: Spot a classic Mickey on the lighthouse behind Old Port Royale.
2 points

Clue 64: Search for a classic Mickey in the children's water play area near the main (Old Port Royale) pool.
4 points

Clue 65: Study the rockwork of the main pool for a classic Mickey. (Psst! Look under a cannon.)
5 points

Clue 66: Walk around just outside the main pool to marvel at this Mickey image.
5 points

Clue 67: In Shutters restaurant, find a classic Mickey in a painting.
4 points

## Downtown Disney Area Resorts
## (94 points)

### ★ *Old Key West Resort* (23 points)

Clue 68: Check the fences in Conch Flats General Store.
2 points

Clue 69: Take a close look at the fence railings in the registration area.
2 points

Clue 70: At the pool, spot a Mickey with a big mouth.
3 points

Clue 71: Find a Hidden Mickey near the steps to the water slide.
4 points

Clue 72: Notice the design of certain railings on the guest buildings outside.
2 points

★ Search for classic Mickeys formed by three shell imprints in the cement on the paths leading from parking spaces to Building 36.

Clue 73: Search the pavement on the right side of the first path for imprints.
5 points

Clue 74: On the second path, explore the corner of the sidewalk after the first right turn.
5 points

(Note: More of these amazing Mickeys may be scattered around Old Key West Resort.)

### ★ *Port Orleans Resort – French Quarter*
(5 points)

Clue 75: Find a classic Mickey in the registration area.
3 points

Clue 76: Look up for a classic Mickey in the food court area.
2 points

### ★ *Port Orleans Resort – Riverside* (11 points)

Clue 77: Look for classic Mickeys in the latticework of the registration area.
2 points

Clue 78: Also in the registration area, find more classic Mickeys near the giant fans.
2 points

Clue 79: Now spot Hidden Mickeys on the fans themselves.
3 points

★ Cross the river and visit Parterre Place.

Clue 80: Find Mickeys outside the Parterre Place building.
4 points for all

★ *Saratoga Springs Resort* (55 points)

Clue 81: Behind the Artist's Palette shop, look around for Mickey on a door handle.
5 points

Clue 82: Notice classic Mickeys on a jacket near The Turf Club.
2 points

Clue 83: Spot Mickey on a gate.
3 points

Clue 84: Find more Mickey images inside on a wall.
2 points for one or more

Clue 85: Look around inside The Turf Club for a classic Mickey on a wall.
3 points

Clue 86: Check out a statue outside the main lobby for three pairs of Hidden Mickeys. (Note: The statue also sports a décor Mickey.)
10 points for finding all six

Clue 87: Search for two Hidden Mickeys near stairs outside the Artist's Palette.
5 points for spotting both

Clue 88: Look for Hidden Mickeys on the outside wall and the downstairs entrance door of the spa.
4 points for spotting both

Clue 89: Admire the guest buildings for small Mickeys.
2 points

Clue 90: Search for a Hidden Mickey on an outdoor wall, near the check-in point.
5 points

Clue 91: Now find a similar Hidden Mickey on a wall in the Congress Park section near the Downtown Disney lagoon.
5 points

Clue 92: Look around for Hidden Mickeys on outdoor wall lights.
4 points

Clue 93: Find classic Mickeys in the Villa courtyards.
2 points

Clue 94: Locate Mickey near the Grandstand Pool.
3 points

## Epcot Resorts (110 points)

To explore the following hotels, park at one and walk around Crescent Lake to the others. Smile and tell the guards that you're searching for Hidden Mickeys.

### ★ *BoardWalk Resort* (41 points)

Clue 95: Spot two classic Mickeys on a horse in the main lobby.
3 points for both

Clue 96: Search for a classic Mickey on a lobby wall.
4 points

Clue 97: Find classic Mickeys on lamps in the lobby.
2 points for one or more

Clue 98: Squint for classic Mickeys above an elephant.
4 points

Clue 99: Look for Mickey near the Villa elevators.
4 points

Clue 100: Check out posters inside elevators for classic Mickeys.
3 points for two or more

Clue 101: Wander around the guestroom and elevator hallways in both the Board-Walk Inn and the BoardWalk Villas. (Note:

these images change or disappear from time to time.)
8 points for four or more different Mickeys
4 more points for a Tinker Bell!

Clue 102: Find Mickey (and his hands!) at an outside bar.
2 points

Clue 103: Look around for a Hidden Mickey near Seashore Sweets.
4 points

Clue 104: Check out the waiting area of Kouzzina Restaurant for a classic Mickey.
3 points

★ *Beach Club Resort* (49 points)

Clue 105: Search for Mickey Mouse along the inside walkway in front of the Cape May Café.
3 points

Clue 106: Look around just inside the entrance to Cape May Café for Mickey on a plate.
4 points

Clue 107: Now search for a crayon Hidden Mickey in this part of the café to earn some bonus points. (Note: this Hidden Image isn't always present.)
3 bonus points

★ Walk to the Beach Club Solarium to find more Hidden Mickeys. (Psst! Check the walls.)

Clue 108: Spot some car tires with Mickey's full face.
3 points

Clue 109: Now look for classic Mickeys in the same general area.
2 points

Clue 110: Gaze at Mickey's face in the sky.
3 points

Clue 111: Search for Mickey on the sand.
4 points

Clue 112: Now find classic Mickeys in the water.
2 points

Clue 113: Do you see other classic Mickeys floating in the air?
2 points

Clue 114: Squint for a Hidden Mickey atop a building.
5 points

Clue 115: Walk to a guestroom hallway to find classic Mickeys under your feet.
2 points for one or more

Clue 116: Now stare at the hallway walls for more.
3 points

Clue 117: Find Mickey in the Marketplace shop.
2 points

Clue 118: Study the area near the entrance to the Beach Club Villas for a classic Mickey.
4 points

Clue 119: Enter The Breezeway in the Beach Club Villas and locate Mickey.
3 points

Clue 120: Wander into the Beaches & Cream Soda Shop to spot a tasty Hidden Mickey on the wall.
4 points

Clue 121: Now watch hamburger preparation on the Beaches & Cream grill for a classic Mickey.
3 points

★ *Yacht Club Resort* (20 points)

Clue 122: Study the globe in the main lobby.
5 points

Clue 123: Look for a cabinet in the main lobby with character names on the drawers.
4 points

**186**

Clue 124: Check out the lobby carpet.
2 points

Clue 125: Check out other resort carpets for Mickeys.
4 points for two or more

Clue 126: In the Yachtsman Steakhouse, look for the photograph of (now deceased) Minnie Moo, a cow born with a black classic Mickey on her side. (You may have to ask a Cast Member where the photo is located. It's sometimes not on public display.)
5 points

## WDW Dolphin Resort (3 points)

Clue 127: Walk into the main lobby and look for classic Mickeys.
3 points

## Fort Wilderness Resort (12 points)

**To explore the Fort Wilderness and Wilderness Lodge Resorts**, take a boat from the Magic Kingdom or from the Contemporary Resort to their respective marinas, or hop on a Disney bus or into your car for transportation to their front entrances.

At Fort Wilderness, you'll need to ride an internal bus between the Hidden Mickeys at the rear near the lake (where your hunt begins) and the Hidden Mickeys near the front parking area.

Clue 128: Visit the Blacksmith (near the Horse Barn) and find a Hidden Mickey.
3 points

Clue 129: Check out Trail's End Restaurant inside for a classic Mickey.
3 points

Clue 130: Go to the Trail Ride Check-In building near the front parking area to find two Hidden Mickeys.
3 points for both

Clue 131: Stroll over to the Fort Wilderness registration building ("Reception Outpost") at the far side of the front parking area and look for Mickey.
3 points

## Wilderness Lodge Resort (118 points)

Clue 132: Check out the signs on the right side of the entrance drive.
2 points

Clue 133: Search out a classic Mickey on the guard-gate kiosk.
3 points

Clue 134: Near the car unloading area, look up for a classic Mickey etched in a support pole above a black metal band.
4 points

Clue 135: Now search for a classic Mickey etched in another support pole and partially hidden under a black metal band.
4 points

Clue 136: Glance down for a tiny classic Mickey traced in the cement on a black stripe.
5 points

Clue 137: Look up again for a classic Mickey etched on a side support pole.
4 points

Clue 138: Find a classic Mickey on a large key in the registration area.
1 point

Clue 139: Look overhead for Mickey driving a bus.
2 points

Clue 140: Find a classic Mickey on the rock of the main lobby fireplace.
5 points

Clue 141: Peek at a fireplace inside the Whispering Canyon Café for a classic Mickey. (Ask a Cast Member to let you into the rear of the café.)
4 points

Clue 142: Look for a classic Mickey on a

wall map at the entrance stairs to the Territory Lounge.
3 points

Clue 143: Now go inside and spot a classic Mickey on a ceiling mural above the bar.
4 points

Clue 144: Inside the Artist Point restaurant, spot a classic Mickey in a large mural above the entrance to the rear left dining area.
4 points

Clue 145: Now scan another mural for a classic Mickey near the restaurant's ceiling. (Psst!: Turn back toward the entrance.)
5 points

Clue 146: Next scan the walls of the restaurant for Winnie the Pooh.
3 points

Clue 147: Search inside the Roaring Fork snack bar for a Hidden Mickey in a display case.
3 points

Clue 148: Find a classic Mickey in one or more lights near the elevators close to the snack bar.
3 points

Clue 149: Glance at the hallway walls for small Hidden Mickeys.
3 points

Clue 150: Look down in the hallways for more.
2 points

Clue 151: Locate a classic Mickey near Room 6100.
3 points

Clue 152: Explore one floor down for a classic Mickey near Room 5066.
3 points

Clue 153: Find another classic near Room 4035.
3 points

Clue 154: Search for a classic Mickey in the rock outside at Fire Rock Geyser.
4 points

Clue 155: Find stairs outside an exit door from the main building (on the side toward the Boat and Bike Rental) and look up for a classic Mickey.
4 points

### ★ *In the Cub's Den* (8 points)

(Tip: Visit in the afternoon if possible. It's less crowded then and the Cast Members are more likely to let you in. Tell them you're searching for Hidden Mickeys.)

Clue 156: Spot a plush Mickey doll in a mural.
2 points

Clue 157: Look higher for a side-profile Mickey.
3 points

Clue 158: Find a classic Mickey in the same mural.
3 points

### ★ *In Wilderness Lodge Villas* (29 points)

Clue 159: Search for four classic Mickeys on a wall near the Wilderness Lodge Villas' lobby. (Psst! look behind some fabric for one of the four.)
5 points for all finding all four

Clue 160: Look around the stone pillars near the Villas lobby for a classic Mickey in the rock.
5 points

Clue 161: Smile back at Mickey hiding in a hole in a beam in the lobby.
5 points

Clue 162: Locate a side profile of Mickey on a wall near the lobby.
4 points

Clue 163: Spot Mickeys around a painting in a room near the lobby.
3 points

Clue 164: Find Mickey in the rock in the Carolwood Pacific Railroad Room near the lobby.
5 points

Clue 165: Look up for Mickey in the hallways of the Widerness Lodge Villas.
2 points

# Magic Kingdom Monorail Resorts
# (148 points)

To find the Hidden Mickeys in these resorts and the nearby Wedding Pavilion, park at the Polynesian or the Grand Floridian and ride the monorail to the other two resorts and past the Wedding Pavilion. Or if you prefer, walk or drive to the Wedding Pavilion. (Note: The Polynesian has the bigger parking lot.)

★ *Polynesian Resort* (48 points)

Clue 166: On the lower level, look for a classic Mickey on the floor near the waterfall.
4 points

Clue 167: Locate four classic Mickeys behind the registration counter. (Tip: They're near each other.)
5 points for all four

Clue 168: Spot three Hidden Mickeys in the Tiki Boutique store.
4 points for finding all three

Clue 169: Search for another just outside the store.
3 points

Clue 170: Check the carpet nearby for classic Mickeys.
3 points for three or more

Clue 171: Study the bamboo-ring wall decorations by the corner staircase.
3 points

★ Find a Hidden Mickey in Trader Jack's gift shop.

Clue 172: Look for a chair on top of a merchandise cabinet.
2 points

Clue 173: Study the nearby carpet.
4 points for two classic Mickeys

Clue 174: Walk by the Kona Café and find a classic Mickey.
2 points

Clue 175: At the Kona Island coffee bar, search for a small classic Mickey.
5 points

Clue 176: Outside on the walkway to the monorail, stare down from the railing for a classic Mickey.
5 points

Clue 177: Look around inside Captain Cook's snack bar for a Hidden Mickey that comes and goes.
5 points

Clue 178: Look down for Hidden Mickeys in hallways and elevators.
3 points for spotting both

★ *Wedding Pavilion* (3 points)

Clue 179: As your monorail car passes by the pavilion buildings, observe the weather vane.
3 points

(Note: A Hidden Mickey may be lurking inside, but the Wedding Pavilion isn't open to the general public.)

★ *Grand Floridian Resort & Spa* (49 points)

Clue 180: Take a good look at the weather vanes on the roofs.
3 points for one or more

Clue 181: Check the large trolley carts outside the hotel.
1 point

Clue 182: Study the lobby carpet.
2 points

Clue 183: Look at the floor tile for a classic Mickey.
2 points

Clue 184: While you're at it, check the tile for the Fab Five.
5 points for five characters

Clue 185: Look near 1900 Park Fare restaurant for a Mickey hat.
3 points

Clue 186: Also near 1900 Park Fare, find Mickey and Minnie below your feet.
2 points for both

Clue 187: Now look for other Disney movie characters, as well as Mickey and Minnie, in the floor encircling the main lobby and in front of the Grand Floridian Café.
5 points for five or more characters

Clue 188: Spot Mickey on the outside of the ornate lobby elevator by the stairs.
4 points

Clue 189: Look up high for Mickey on the ceiling above the main lobby.
4 points

Clue 190: Check out the classic Mickey in front of the M. Mouse Mercantile shop.
1 point

Clue 191: Find Hidden Mickeys in the hallway walls.
2 points for one or more

Clue 192: Now look down for others in the hallways.
2 points

Clue 193: Locate two classic Mickeys on a picture inside Gasparilla Grill & Games.
4 points for spotting both

Clue 194: Locate a classic Mickey near the checkout counters.
3 points

Clue 195: Find Mickey and other characters in the lobbies of the outer buildings.
4 points for four or more

Clue 196: Walk into the Grand Floridian Convention Center's main entrance and look around for Mickey.
2 points

★ *Contemporary Resort* (48 points*)
   *including Bay Lake Tower

Clue 197: From the window of the California Grill restaurant, on the top floor, spot a stretched out Mickey watchband on the ground in front of the hotel.
4 points

Clue 198: Check out the (closed) glass doors of the back room inside the California Grill restaurant. (If the doors are open, you may not see the Hidden Mickey.)
4 points

Clue 199: Go to the sixth floor and walk in the direction of the Transportation and Ticket Center to an outside balcony to spot this amazing Hidden Mickey. (Tip: This Mickey can also be seen from the monorails.)
5 points

Clue 200: Look for Mickey's profile inside Chef Mickey's restaurant.
1 point

Clue 201: Check out some classic Mickeys on a shelf inside Chef Mickey's.
2 points

Clue 202: Don't miss Mickey's ears at the rear of Chef Mickey's!
3 points

Clue 203: Find Mickey on a wall near Contempo Café.
3 points

Clue 204: Look high for a classic Mickey on an animal.
4 points

Clue 205: Search for a stick figure Mickey near the shops.
3 points

Clue 206: Look for classic Mickeys in The Game Station Arcade.
3 points for all

Clue 207: Find a classic Mickey silhouette in the bricks behind the main hotel. (Psst! It's near Mickey Mouse himself.)
2 points

Clue 208: Locate a Hidden Mickey in The Sand Bar.
3 points

Clue 209: Spot Mickey in the tile at the exit from the Garden Building to the parking lot.
5 points

Clue 210: Look up for Mickey at the hotel entrance.
2 points

★ *Bay Lake Tower* (4 points)

Clue 211: Walk to Bay Lake Tower and locate Mickey from the outside. (Psst!: Look high!)
4 points

## Shades of Green Resort (9 points)

(Only folks with military connections are allowed into this resort.)

Clue 212: Search for four classic Mickeys in the lobby.
5 points for finding all four

Clue 213: Find a large classic Mickey outside (or on a map of the resort).
4 points

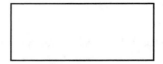

## Total Points for Hotel Hunt =

### How'd you do?

A perfect score for this scavenger hunt is 721. But you may have done even better if you earned bonus points in the Cape May Café or by spotting Hidden Characters on the WDW buses. Here is a point breakdown by resort and resort group, so that you can compare your score with the perfect score for the areas you've covered. You'll find the total points for each section in parentheses. Give yourself Gold if you scored at least 80% of the points available, Bronze if you scored at least 40%.

**Animal Kingdom Lodge Resort (107)**
    Kidani Village (27)
**Disney's All-Star Resorts (16)**
    All-Star Sports Resort (7)
    All-Star Music Resort (5)
    All-Star Movies Resort (4)
**Coronado Springs Resort (38)**
**Pop Century Resort (43)**
**Caribbean Beach Resort (23)**
**Downtown Disney Area Resorts (94)**
    Old Key West Resort (23)
    Port Orleans Resort – French Quarter (5)
    Port Orleans Resort – Riverside (11)
    Saratoga Springs Resort (55)
**Epcot Resorts (110)**
    BoardWalk Resort (41)
    Beach Club Resort (49)
    Yacht Club Resort (20)
**WDW Dolphin Resort (3)**
**Fort Wilderness Resort (12)**
**Wilderness Lodge Resort (118)**
**Magic Kingdom Monorail Resorts (148)**
    Polynesian Resort (48)
        Wedding Pavilion (3)

        Grand Floridian Resort & Spa (49)
        Contemporary Resort (48)
       **Shades of Green (9)**

**Caution:
Don't peek at this
section unless you
really want help!**

## Animal Kingdom Lodge Resort

Hint 1: Outside, above the lower roof, the second tall figure to the left of the car baggage drop-off area has a classic Mickey in his mouth.

Hint 2: On the right wall mural between the outer and inner entrance doors to the main lobby, an orange and brown creature sports a classic Mickey in a circle on its mid back.

Hint 3: Inside the main lobby, you can find a classic Mickey near the bottom of the second chandelier on the right (as you face in from the front entrance). The Hidden Mickey is near the bottom of one of the shields.

Hint 4: Around the main lobby, classic Mickeys are formed by logs banded to wood supports. One of the best is the second support on the right (as you enter the lobby from the front doors). It's on the second level, on the side away from the main lobby entrance.

197

Hint 5: On the right side of the main lobby (as you face in from the front entrance), a short bridge crosses a rockbound pool of water. A classic Mickey is visible on the rock from the side of the bridge nearest the lobby. It's toward the rear on the right side. To spot it, look for the first recess in the rock from the right edge of the pool. Mickey is at the back of this recess, above the water line.

Hint 6: Go down the staircase at the rear of the lobby. Turn left and walk down the Kudu Trail hallway. In the first small lobby, near the elevator, a classic Mickey is on the top end of a piece of wood that's roped to two giant "log" supports. Mickey is above the second rope binding, near the ceiling.

Hint 7: Outside the rear doors of the main lobby, a green Mickey in side profile hides in the decorative vines to the right as you exit. He is about two-thirds of the way up the side of the vine-covered column, above the middle horizontal brace. Look for him at the top of an open space in the vines. He's looking into the lobby.

Hint 8: Outside the rear exit from the main lobby, on the left side of the trail to Arusha Rock Overlook, check the rock wall for a decorative relief of a group of giraffes. You'll find a classic Mickey among the spots on the middle of the large giraffe in the center, above the inner front leg.

Hint 9: Along the walkway in Arusha Rock Overlook, a rock sports a classic Mickey. Look for it where the trail first turns left between rock walls. It's on the right side in the first small alcove, about six feet up from the path and under a large overhanging rock.

Hint 10: Toward the bottom of the staircase that winds from the right side of the main lobby to Boma restaurant, there's a classic Mickey on the rock wall next to a waterfall.

Hint 11: Inside Boma, you'll see classic Mickeys on some of the chairs with tall metal backs.

 Hint 12: Inside Jiko restaurant, a classic Mickey is formed on the ceiling above the

two large orange oven exhausts and the white column behind them.

Hint 13: From the entrance to Jiko, walk to the third table on your left, next to the glass windows. Outside in the shallow pool area, a classic Mickey is sculpted on the first rock island from the left that has a pillar jutting out of it.

Hint 14: Outside the exit from the restaurants, a large rock on the left side of the path behind the water slide has a classic Mickey impressed on its lower half near the ground. The rock is about three-quarters of the way along the walkway to the water slide. A small light pole juts out of the top of this rock.

Hint 15: A light-colored classic Mickey is cut into a rock wall behind the swimming pool. The wall forms the back of the pool's water slide. The Mickey is several feet above the walkway, below a gazebo that marks the starting point for the water slide.

Hint 16: Walk behind the pool to the bird and flamingo overlook. From the rightmost "Bird Spotter Guide" on the fence along the main trail, look to your right to the opposite fence. About two-thirds of the distance along this fence from the main trail, a pinkish classic Mickey with a white right ear is about one foot down from the top of the rock.

Hint 17: A Mickey image is etched in the cement outside of The Mara restaurant. Go to the walkway leading to the pool, which is directly opposite the rear exit door from the restaurant. Near the end of this short walkway, and on the left side as you stroll toward the pool, you'll find the Hidden Mickey.

Hint 18: A classic stone Mickey is on the rear of the short wall behind The Mara seating area. It's about three feet up from the ground, behind an emergency phone and a tall brown pole.

Hint 19: In the food area of The Mara, a classic Mickey is on the upper left wall in the third leaf from the left tree (in the mural of falling leaves).

Hint 20: Above the bakery, on the mural with green foliage, a tiny green classic Mickey is hiding just above the bottom rim, facing the wine cabinet.

Hint 21: Also in the food area, a classic Mickey hides in a leaf in the middle of the upper right mural of falling leaves.

Hint 22: As you enter the elevator to the Fitness Center, you can spot a classic Mickey on the lower left panel (as you face the rear of the elevator).

Hint 23: Many small classic Mickeys can be found in the carpet in the hallways in front of guestrooms. Classic Mickey images in the carpets below the fifth floor differ from those on and above the fifth floor.

Hint 24: On the third floor, at the end of the first short hall to the right of the main Zebra Trail hallway, an upside-down classic Mickey is formed by three plates on a wall.

### -Kidani Village

Hint 25: A classic Mickey is at the 6:30 position on a large gold clock on a table just inside the entrance.

Hint 26: A white classic Mickey is on a ladybug on the middle level of the closest chandelier to the front lobby entrance.

Hint 27: At the entrance to Sanaa restaurant downstairs, a classic Mickey made of baskets is on the wall behind the check-in desk.

Hint 28: Inside Sanaa restaurant, a classic Mickey is above a booth on a white wall. It is to the left as you enter.

Hint 29: Classic Mickeys hide in the woodwork in the middle of Sanaa's dining tables.

Hint 30: Outside Sanaa, a classic Mickey is etched on the rockwork at the bottom rear of the lobby stairs.

Hint 31: Many small classic Mickeys can be found in the carpet in the hallways in front of guest-rooms.

(Other Hidden Mickeys are in the Spa and Health Club area, but generally only Kidani Village guests are allowed to enter there.)

# Disney's All-Star Resorts

### -All-Star Sports Resort

Hint 32: In the main building gift shop, classic Mickeys are part of the carpet. Each is composed of a baseball with two circles for ears.

Hint 33: In The Market food court order area, a black classic Mickey is on the clock on the right wall behind the clock's hands.

Hint 34: Outside, behind and to the right of the registration building, and past the buildings with surfboards, a large Mickey statue stands directly over a classic Mickey (white head and black ears) in the cement.

### -All-Star Music Resort

Hint 35: In the Jazz Inn courtyard, classic Mickey ears top the cymbal stands. Each is a winged nut that holds a cymbal in place. (These nuts come and go.)

Hint 36: In the Country Fair area, you'll find classic Mickeys on the front and back of the huge boots.

### -All-Star Movies Resort

Hint 37: On a mural in an outside display window in front of the gift shop next to the lobby, a small black classic Mickey hides at the lower right of the mural. He's on the front of an orange book with the title "Future Plans."

Hint 38: The large checkers in Andy's Room in the "Toy Story" section sport classic Mickeys.

## Coronado Springs Resort

Hint 39: At the front entrance to the main lobby, a medallion on the upper left of the left large, open wooden door is a three-dimensional relief of Mickey's face.

Hint 40: On the wider part of the stone seating that surrounds the lobby fountain, a classic Mickey image is shaded slightly darker than the color of the stone. It's on the right side of the fountain (as you enter the lobby), near the front of the seating area and next to a short pole in the water.

Hint 41: A tiny red classic Mickey is embedded in the middle of the floor at the entrance to the registration area.

Hint 42: A three-dimensional Mickey face is on the large right wooden door (as you face the doors) at the exit labeled El Centro.

Hint 43: In the hallway outside the Veracruz Exhibit Hall in the Convention Center, a black classic Mickey pattern repeats along the sides of some of the ceiling chandeliers. Nearby, a similar Mickey pattern can be spotted on rectangular light covers that are flush with the ceiling.

Hint 44: A classic Mickey is chipped into the cement next to the lamppost nearest the Marina rental gazebo.

Hint 45: At the Dig Site swimming pool's main entrance (closest to the lake), a classic Mickey hides on a wall to your right. To spot him, check out the upper middle part of the wall facing the lake before you enter the Dig Site.

Hint 46: After you enter the Dig Site, examine the wall to your left (as you enter) that faces the pool. A classic Mickey is on the upper left side.

Hint 47: Also at the Dig Site, you'll find a whitish, somewhat distorted classic Mickey near the very top of the Mayan pyramid, on the side facing the pool. It's on the second stone block from the left, fourth row from the top.

Hint 48: To the left of the restrooms at the Dig Site, a circular stone tablet with relief images is hanging on the wall. A somewhat distorted sideways classic Mickey hides at the lower right.

Hint 49: Mickey Mouse (side profile) is sitting in a bus on some of the bus stop signs located around the periphery of the resort (such as at Bus Stops No. 2, No. 3, and No. 4).

## Pop Century Resort

Hint 50: In a small TV room near the check-in area, classic Mickey bubbles are under a fish in a fishbowl painted on the wall.

Hint 51: In a photograph on the wall behind the middle of the long registration counter, a classic Mickey formed of moon craters is at the lower right of a television screen.

Hint 52: In the shop near the food court, classic Mickey holes are in the poles that hold merchandise racks.

Hint 53: Inside the food court seating area, classic Mickeys made of circles can be found on the undulating purple, brown, blue, and green divider walls.

Hint 54: Several classic Mickeys are hiding on the tile floor of the food court order area. One is in the center of the order and pay area. Another is in front of the middle cash register.

Hint 55: Inside the gift shop, near the exit to the bus stop, check the wall behind the cash registers to spot round gift boxes that

203

form a classic Mickey. The image appears twice in faux package-locker windows. One image is in the second window from the top of the second column of windows from the right side. The other is in the third window from the left along the top row.

Hint 56: Behind Roger Rabbit, in a mural on one of the '80s buildings near the Computer Pool, a classic Mickey is at the top of a bush beside a building. The bush's topmost leaf is just above Mickey's head and ears.

Hint 57: Two black classic Mickeys are on the keyboard of the huge computer near the Computer Pool. Both are on the lower row of keys. One is on the second key from the left and the other is on the second key from the right. (More obvious decorative classic Mickeys are in the computer monitor's screensaver.)

Hint 58: Look sharp for a lightly traced classic Mickey in green paint on an outside wall of the '60s building, behind the Mowgli figure and just past the Hippy Dippy Pool. It's on the left side of the wall with green plants, about halfway up the wall, above a leaf and to the right of a brown tree.

Hint 59: In the guest laundry rooms near both the Hippy Dippy Pool and the Bowling Pool, bubbles form two sideways classic Mickeys. You'll find them in the same places in both laundry rooms. One is on the lower right front of the soap vending machine and the other is at the upper right.

Hint 60: "Mickey Mouse Club March" is choice "C2" on the giant jukebox near the Bowling Pool. ("I've Got a Date at Disneyland" is choice "F10.")

Hint 61: Outside the main lobby, classic Mickeys are at the ends of the guardrails near the bus stops.

## Caribbean Beach Resort

Hint 62: Outside the main entrance to Old Port Royale from the parking lot, you'll find a display for Shutters restaurant on the left wall. In the lower right photo in the display, three blueberries form a classic Mickey.

Hint 63: Behind Old Port Royale, a classic Mickey appears in the "Barefoot Bay Boat Yard" sign on the side of the lighthouse near the bike racks.

Hint 64: In the child's water play area near the main pool, a classic Mickey is on the helm near the wheel of the pirate ship.

Hint 65: At the main swimming pool, a tan classic Mickey is on the rockwork of the small slide's wall. To spot it, stand at the back of the pool and look under the left cannon. Mickey is on a long rock in the second row of rocks from the bottom. This great Mickey image has almost faded away.

Hint 66: Where the sidewalk from Trinidad North meets the sidewalk outside the main (Old Port Royale) pool, they are joined by a short sidewalk that takes you to the right toward the main resort parking area. As you face the parking area from this intersection, look down at the lower right corner of the first white cement section of the short sidewalk. A small classic Mickey is etched in the pavement not far from a green lamppost.

Hint 67: In Shutters restaurant, a cloud classic Mickey is in a painting on the left wall of the room close to the rear exit door.

## Downtown Disney Area Resorts

### -Old Key West Resort

Hint 68: Throughout Conch Flats General Store, the design in the fence woodwork includes classic Mickeys.

Hint 69: Classic Mickeys are worked into the design of the fence railings behind the check-in counter in the registration area.

Hint 70: At the main pool (behind the registration building), the water slide (hidden in the rock) opens into the pool through the head of a classic Mickey.

Hint 71: At the upper right of the entrance

to the steps to the water slide, a classic Mickey is indented in the white rock, above a space in the wall.

Hint 72: You'll see classic Mickeys in the outdoor railings around the guest buildings.

Hints 73 and 74: Classic Mickeys formed by three shell imprints in the cement can be found on the two paths leading from parking spaces to Building 36. On the first path, you'll find the Hidden Mickey just after the first right turn on the right side. On the second path, the three shell imprints are in the corner of the sidewalk, after the first right turn and just before the next left turn.

### -Port Orleans Resort – French Quarter

Hint 75: On the third painting from the left behind the registration counter, an upside-down classic Mickey is on a man's crown.

Hint 76: Upside-down classic Mickeys made of blue and white gemstones adorn the top of a crown hanging from the ceiling on the right side of the food court seating area.

### -Port Orleans Resort – Riverside

Hint 77: Above the registration area, classic Mickeys are repeated in the wooden latticework circling the central lobby.

Hint 78: In the registration area, classic Mickeys decorate the sides of the brackets that hold the giant fans hanging from the ceiling above the center of the lobby.

Hint 79: Classic Mickeys are at the base of the strapping on the big ceiling fans.

Hint 80: Small classic Mickeys are in the upper level side rails at Parterre Place.

### -Saratoga Springs Resort

Hint 81: Halfway down the hallway behind the Artist's Palette Shop (turn right as you enter the shop from the main lobby), a

full-body impression of Mickey Mouse swinging a golf club is on a handle on the left door.

Hint 82: In the hallway leading to The Turf Club Bar and Grill, the jacket in a display on the left wall sports black classic Mickeys.

Hint 83: Just before entering the lounge area in front of The Turf Club, notice the small, ornate gate to your right, near The Turf Club menu posted on the brick wall. Examine the right half of the gate. Three small blue circles in the left middle area form a classic Mickey image tilted sideways to the left. (This image is not proportioned perfectly, but many guests and Cast Members like this image as a Hidden Mickey.)

Hint 84: On a wall inside the lounge in front of The Turf Club, Mickey and other Disney characters decorate billiard balls. They are in the first display to the left as you enter from the hallway.

Hint 85: In a left wall display just inside the dining area of The Turf Club, three circles on equestrian equipment form an upside-down classic Mickey.

Hint 86: On a statue of a horse and rider outside the main lobby, the rings attaching the bridle to the reins and bit on both sides of the horse's mouth form classic Mickeys. Tiny classic Mickeys are also hidden in the roses on both sides of the horse's winner's blanket. You'll find them in the middle of the blanket in about the third or fourth row down. Finally, large blue classic Mickeys decorate the back and front of the jockey's jersey. (In addition, a blanket on the horse includes a yellow décor Mickey.)

Hint 87: As you walk away from the Artist's Palette, look for depressions in the left rock wall at the top of the stairs to the High Rock Spring Pool. One classic Mickey is in the middle of the top horizontal rock of the wall, and a second classic Mickey is on the lower horizontal rock near the handrail post.

Hint 88: Small classic Mickeys adorn the

spa signs on the wall outside and on the glass door at the downstairs spa entrance.

Hint 89: Some balcony railings on the guest buildings have classic Mickey holes.

Hint 90: In the resort's Springs section (Villas 4101 – 4436), across from the check-in parking lot, a large faint classic Mickey is on an outdoor red wall.

Hint 91: In the resort's Congress Park section (Villas 1501 – 1836), near the lagoon over which you can see Downtown Disney, another large faint classic Mickey is on an outdoor red wall. I stood near this red wall and could spot the Rainforest Café across the lagoon.

Hint 92: Classic Mickeys can be found in the upper corners of some of the outside lights on the guest buildings, such as on the exterior of the enclosed stairways.

Hint 93: Classic Mickeys are at the bottom of obelisks in the Villa courtyards.

Hint 94: Partial classic Mickeys are in the left side of the gate to the Grandstand pool and on the back gate next to the restrooms.

# Epcot Resorts

### -BoardWalk Resort

Hint 95: In the main lobby, an outside horse on the small carousel has brown spots that form two classic Mickeys, one on the neck and one on the thigh.

Hint 96: In the middle painting on the wall above the middle registration counter in the main lobby, a classic Mickey is formed by the second small group of trees from the right.

Hint 97: Classic Mickeys hold the shades in place on the lamps facing the fireplace in the center of the lobby.

Hint 98: Along a side wall inside the lobby,

tiny classic Mickey holes are at the very tops of the red latticework designs on all sides of the canopied seat (called a "howdah") atop the elephant.

Hint 99: On the first to the fifth floors of the BoardWalk Villas, a classic Mickey sits atop light fixtures alongside the elevators.

Hint 100: Classic Mickeys of different colors are usually hiding around the edges and in the background of some of the posters in BoardWalk Resort elevators.

Hint 101: Classic Mickeys hide in the carpet in front of some elevators and also appear in the lobby carpets and the guestroom hallway carpets in both the BoardWalk Inn and BoardWalk Villas. Also on the Inn and Villas' carpets, you'll find Tinker Bell in front of elevators.

Hint 102: Walk outside behind the BoardWalk Villas to the Leaping Horse Libations pool bar to spot a classic Mickey at the top of the wall clock behind the bar counter. Mickey's hands tell you the time.

Hint 103: On the sign over the entrance to Seashore Sweets, a cloud classic Mickey is in the sky between the two ladies, next to the head of the lady on the left.

Hint 104: As you enter the waiting room for Kouzzina Restaurant, look at the right wall behind the check-in counter for a classic Mickey made of plates.

### -Beach Club Resort

Hint 105: Along the inside walkway in front of the Cape May Café, a full length Mickey Mouse is standing in a sandcastle. It's the sculpture farthest to the left, on the wall facing the pool.

Hint 106: A classic Mickey is on a blue plate inside Cape May Café. The plate is perched on a small shelf on the right wall just past the check-in podium at the restaurant's entrance. Mickey is on the inside of the plate and has a red circle for a "head" and two black circles for his "ears." The plate is evidently rotated from time to time, as this classic Mickey is sometimes upside down.

Hint 107: At Cape May Café, a display on the wall just inside the restaurant sometimes includes a Hidden Mickey or other Hidden Characters made of crayons. These images change from time to time.

Hint 108: Enter the Solarium from the Beach Club main lobby. The first painting on the wall to your left has Mickey's face on spare tires on the backs of the yellow car (left side) and the blue car (right side).

Hint 109: Classic Mickey hood ornaments adorn the blue and red cars on the right of this painting.

Hint 110: In the second painting on the left wall, you can see Mickey's face looking out at you from the clouds at the upper right.

Hint 111: In this second painting, a lady on the beach is sitting on a Mickey Mouse towel.

Hint 112: The cruise ship smokestacks in this second painting have classic Mickey decals.

Hint 113: Mickey balloons are on the right side of the third painting to your left.

Hint 114: Also on the right side of this third painting is a tiny white classic Mickey atop the front post of a small building with a brown roof.

Hint 115: The guestroom hallways have carpet segments with classic Mickeys.

Hint 116: Classic Mickeys are in the wallpaper along the guestroom hallways.

Hint 117: Sand dollars form classic Mickeys in the carpet of the Marketplace shop.

Hint 118: Under the Ariel statue in front of the entrance to the Beach Club Villas, seashells are embedded in the ground. One group of three shells forms a classic Mickey.

Hint 119: A hot air Mickey balloon is in a painting found in The Breezeway at the Beach Club Villas. It's on the left wall as you enter The Breezeway from the front doors.

Hint 120: In the Beaches & Cream Soda Shop, onion rings form a classic Mickey. He's on the left wall as you enter, on the second panel back from the rear wall.

Hint 121: You can spot classic Mickey holes in the hamburger press used at the Beaches & Cream Soda Shop to hold the burgers on the hot griddle.

### -Yacht Club Resort

Hint 122: On the globe in the main lobby, a blue classic Mickey is at the bottom right-hand corner of the sea monster, under the sea monster's head and below the island of Madagascar.

Hint 123: In a seating area in the main lobby, the names of Mickey, Minnie, Donald, Daisy, Goofy, and Huey are on small labels on the drawers of a corner cabinet. (This cabinet is moved around at times to different parts of the lobby.)

Hint 124: Near the main lobby seating area, dark classic Mickeys are in the rug.

Hint 125: Various other classic Mickey images can be found in other carpets around the resort, especially near elevators and in the guest hallways.

Hint 126: A photo of (now deceased) Minnie Moo, a cow born with a black classic Mickey on her side, often hangs in the Yachtsman Steakhouse. Examine the left wall just past the entrance podium. Minnie Moo once resided at Fort Wilderness.

# WDW Dolphin Resort

Hint 127: Walk toward the piano in the main lobby and observe the backs of the brown chairs nearby. Several classic Mickeys are formed by wooden circles on the chair backs.

# Fort Wilderness Resort

Hint 128: A classic Mickey brand is on the left side of the Blacksmith sign near the Horse Barn.

Hint 129: Inside Trail's End Restaurant, a classic Mickey is made of frying pans hanging from hooks on the wall behind the food serving station.

Hint 130: At the front parking lot, two Hidden Mickeys are on the Tri-Circle-D Ranch sign on the small Trail Ride Check-In building. They are in the middle of the scrollwork at both sides of the sign.

Hint 131: Inside the Fort Wilderness registration building ("Reception Outpost") at the far side of the main parking lot, a plush Mickey Mouse stands in a metal jug at the far left of a shelf directly over the registration counter.

# Wilderness Lodge Resort

Hint 132: On the right side of the entrance drive to the hotel, a full length Mickey Mouse is walking on top of the "Bear Crossing" sign.

Hint 133: A classic Mickey is on the slanted end of the first horizontal log beam of the guard gate kiosk as your car approaches the entrance gate.

Hint 134: As you approach the center steps from the parking lot, you'll see that the roof of the covered unloading area in front of the entrance is supported by huge wooden logs, banded together (four to a set) by black metal strips. The right rear pole of the first set to the right (as you face the entrance) has a classic Mickey etched in the wood above the upper black metal band. This Mickey faces the parking lot.

Hint 135: In the set of support poles on the left after you walk up the center steps from the parking lot, the pole in the corner closest to you and the hotel entrance has a classic Mickey etched in the wood. This Mickey is partially covered by the upper black metal band; only his head and part of his right ear are visible. This Mickey faces the steps.

Hint 136: In the cement of the car entrance drive-through, the black stripe nearest the center steps from the parking lot has a tiny classic Mickey. From the red rectangle in the cement, follow the right (as you face the hotel entrance) diagonal crack to the black stripe. The tiny classic Mickey is traced in the cement about six inches to the right of the intersection of the crack and the stripe.

Hint 137: As you face the hotel entrance, the left rear support pole of the far left set of poles closest to the parking lot has a classic Mickey etched in the wood. It's above the lateral crossbeam on the lower part of the pole.

Hint 138: A classic Mickey hides on the left side of a large key in a wall display behind the registration counter. Look near the entrance to the Mercantile Shop.

Hint 139: A sign that says "Walt Disney World Transportation" hangs from the ceiling near the Mercantile Shop. Mickey (in side profile) is driving the bus at the top of the sign.

Hint 140: In the lobby, you'll find a classic Mickey on the rock in the corner to the upper right of the fireplace. Search at the level of and near the lower round wooden horizontal beam that juts toward the lobby.

Hint 141: The outer grillwork of a fireplace in the rear room of the Whispering Canyon Café is adorned with decorative cutouts. Bend down low and look for a classic Mickey on the bottom row. It is the third cutout from the left corner.

Hint 142: At the entrance stairs to the Territory Lounge, a classic Mickey decorates a pot in the right lower section of a wall map.

Hint 143: Inside the Territory Lounge, you'll find a classic Mickey on the rear of a beige mule in a ceiling mural. Look above the center of the bar.

Hint 144: Inside the Artist Point restaurant, examine the large mural above the entrance to the rear left dining area. You can spot a classic Mickey in the upper part of the lowest tree on the right if you look between the third and fourth lights (counting from the left) illuminating the mural.

Hint 145: Turn left toward the Artist Point entrance and study the large mural near the ceiling and between the two front sections of the restaurant. On the clothing at the lower back of the leftmost of four horsemen is a light brown classic Mickey, tilted slightly to the right.

Hint 146: Inside the rear left dining area, the top middle part of a dark cloud in a painting on the left wall is shaped like a side profile of Winnie the Pooh. He's looking to the right.

Hint 147: A display case on an inside wall facing the entrance to the Roaring Fork snack bar contains three chestnuts arranged to form a classic Mickey.

Hint 148: You'll find classic Mickey images on a few of the wall-light covers, most often as a sideways image at the lower center of the light cover. Some of these covers are near the elevators just past Roaring Fork snack area. One or more can be found elsewhere around the hotel.

Hint 149: The wallpaper in the guest hallways on most floors (for example, near the elevators) includes classic Mickeys in the design.

Hint 150: Segments of the guest hallway carpets contain blue classic Mickeys.

Hint 151: A classic Mickey is etched near the bottom of a flat vertical wooden post around the corner from Room 6100 and near a green EXIT sign.

Hint 152: Near room 5066, a classic Mickey is etched on a flat vertical wooden post about five and a half feet from the floor. It's across from an ice machine.

Hint 153: A classic Mickey is etched on a vertical wooden post about six feet up from the floor across from Room 4035.

Hint 154: Outside, from the walkway next to Fire Rock Geyser, scan the shallow stream running down from the small pool by the geyser. You'll find a slightly distorted classic Mickey with white rocks for ears in the rock of the streambed about a third of the way up to the geyser.

Hint 155: Walk toward the Boat and Bike Rental and locate stairs to an exit door in the corner of the main building. A classic Mickey is imprinted in a vertical wooden beam at the left side of the exit door (as you face the door) across from the fourth-floor balcony. Mickey is on the right side of the beam, just below the log that juts out to the right.

### -In the Cub's Den

Hint 156: A plush Mickey doll sits in the rightmost teepee in the mural on the right wall.

Hint 157: In this same mural, a side-profile shadow of Mickey (standing and looking right) falls on the side of a mountain to the right of the center of the mural and above the tree line.

Hint 158: On the far left of this mural, about midway up and left of the mountains, you can spot a classic Mickey.

### -Wilderness Lodge Villas

Hint 159: Near the lobby elevators to the left of the entrance to the Villas, four classic Mickeys hide on the wall. One is to the right of the elevators near the lower left corner of a picture frame. Two more are part of the wall decoration between the elevators, and a fourth can be found to the left of the leftmost elevator. This last Mickey is hiding behind the red tapestry.

Hint 160: A classic Mickey made of depressions in the rock is on the last stone pillar to your left as you enter the Villas. You can spot this image just before you step into the lobby. Mickey is about three feet from the floor, on the corner (facing the entrance) of the second horizontal rock from the floor. He is tilted to the right.

Hint 161: Mickey Mouse is peeking out of a hole on the outer side of the first overhead beam to your right as you enter the lobby of the Wilderness Lodge Villas. The beam is jutting out into the lobby and has a rattlesnake on top.

Hint 162: A side profile of Mickey Mouse is on the upper part of a wall, between two moons, near the lobby of the Wilderness Lodge Villas and to the right as you enter the lobby.

Hint 163: Examine the art hanging in the first room to the right after you pass through the Villas' lobby entrance doors. A painting that's hanging on the room's right wall has a frame with classic Mickeys in the corners.

Hint 164: Walk to your right (as you face the Villas lobby) to the Carolwood Pacific Railroad Room. On the left side of the fireplace, a classic Mickey is embedded into the stonework at about the height of the fireplace mantel.

Hint 165: High along the hallways of the Villas, you'll find classic Mickey corner brackets.

## Magic Kingdom Monorail Resorts

### -Polynesian Resort

Hint 166: On the lower level, just inside the main lobby, there's a classic Mickey design in the flagstone tiles a few feet in front of the waterfall.

Hint 167: A painting of a rocky shore with red flowers hangs on the right side of the wall behind the registration counter. Four classic Mickeys are in the painting: one white one in the middle of the painting, another white one at the middle left, one brown one just to the left of the middle of the painting, and an upside-down brown one near the left middle.

Hint 168: Inside the Tiki Boutique store on the first floor and near the various entrances, three wooden statues holding merchandise are adorned with classic Mickeys. Two of the Mickeys are blue and white while the third is red.

Hint 169: A slightly distorted green classic Mickey image is on the upper back of the Tiki statue outside Tiki Boutique. Many folks stop here for photos with the smiling Tiki guy.

Hint 170: Several different classic Mickeys are in the carpet on the first floor near the Wyland Galleries of Florida shop and to the right of the gallery entrance.

Hint 171: Along the right rear corner staircase from the lobby, bamboo wall decorations are composed of rings. Seen end on, some of the lower rings in the decoration on the right side form classic Mickeys.

Hint 172: In Trader Jack's gift shop, Mickey Mouse is sitting in a chair in front of the upper wall mural and on top of some merchandise cabinets. Classic Mickeys are on the arms of his chair.

Hint 173: In the carpet on the second floor near and to the right of Trader Jack's shop, a brown classic Mickey is in the border and a blue classic Mickey is on a turtle shell. A similar carpet with these two Hidden Mickeys is in the kids' craft area on the first floor near the front entrance.

Hint 174: The carpeting on the floor of the Kona Café includes many flowers. Some of the flowers contain classic Mickeys of different colors. You can see these

217

carpet images from the railing outside the Café.

Hint 175: At the Kona Island coffee bar, in front of the Kona Café, small purple tiles on top of the mosaic tile counter form a classic Mickey. You'll spot it to the left of the glass case.

Hint 176: Go outside to the second level walkway to the monorail and look down from the right railing. About halfway from the monorail exit doors to the monorail loading platform, a classic Mickey is formed by three light gray rocks placed on a larger rock in the water. (Heavy rains can move the rocks around at times.)

Hint 177: On the "Order Here" screen at Captain Cook's snack bar, images pan from right to left. As the image moves right, look for a palm tree with Mickey's shadow on its trunk.

Hint 178: The carpet in some of the hallways and elevators sports classic Mickeys.

### -Wedding Pavilion

Hint 179: The weather vane on top of the building closest to the monorail has a full-length side profile of Mickey Mouse.

### -Grand Floridian Resort & Spa

Hint 180: Weather vanes on various roofs at the front of the resort sport classic Mickeys.

Hint 181: The large trolley carts outside the hotel have classic Mickeys in the woodwork around the luggage storage areas at the back of the carts.

Hint 182: In the main lobby, gold classic Mickeys are in the carpet.

Hint 183: Green classic Mickeys are in the corners of the marble tile designs on the floors of the first and second levels of the main building.

218

Hint 184: You'll find the Fab Five Disney characters (Mickey, Minnie, Pluto, Donald and Goofy) in the tile floor near the main lobby's front entrance—and directly above in the tile on the second floor entrance from the monorail.

Hint 185: Along the entrance hall to 1900 Park Fare restaurant, a Mickey hat image is at the left lower corner of the left lower picture in a group of carousel pictures on the wall.

Hint 186: Minnie is here with Mickey (green full-body images) on the tile floor of the foyer in front of the dining area of the 1900 Park Fare restaurant.

Hint 187: Other Disney movie characters are in the tile floor encircling the main lobby and in front of the Grand Floridian Café. They include Tinker Bell, Cinderella and Prince Charming, Peter Pan and friends, Mrs. Potts, and Chip, and of course Mickey and Minnie.

Hint 188: Ornate ironwork encloses the lobby elevators, and the decorative sections between the floors host multiple classic Mickeys. You'll find four classic Mickeys in each ironwork panel at the intersection of the diagonal spokes and the large circle. The ears are oriented toward the center. (Tip: Stand inside the main lobby elevator for the best view of these classic Mickeys.)

Hint 189: Classic Mickey designs are at the bottom of four tall blue flowers in the round stained-glass dome above the main lobby of the Grand Floridian.

Hint 190: On the second floor, a classic Mickey is on the top of a pole on the M. Mouse Mercantile sign in front of the shop.

Hint 191: Most guestroom hallways have classic Hidden Mickeys in the wallpaper.

Hint 192: Classic Mickeys are also in the guest hallway carpets.

Hint 193: Inside Gasparilla Grill & Games, two classic Mickey images are in the third

**219**

picture on the wall to the left, above the restrooms. One is formed by a coin and two rings; the other is on a silver utensil.

Hint 194: Also inside Gasparilla Grill & Games, braces beneath the shelves at the checkout counters are shaped as classic Mickeys.

Hint 195: In the lobbies of the outer guest buildings, the carpets have Hidden Mickeys as well as a Hidden Minnie Mouse, Donald Duck, Goofy, and Pluto.

Hint 196: Step into the main entrance area of the Grand Floridian Convention Center and look up for a hot air Mickey balloon painted on the ceiling.

### -Contemporary Resort

Hint 197: From the window of the California Grill restaurant on the hotel's top floor, you can see a stretched out Mickey watchband on the ground in front of the building. It's among the conical-shaped trees. (You can see part of this watchband from the monorail.)

Hint 198: Inside the California Grill, the top of a classic Mickey is frosted in the design of the (closed) glass doors of the back room.

Hint 199: From the sixth floor outdoor balcony closest to the front of the hotel, look left to see Mickey sitting on the edge of a roof below! This Mickey can also be spotted from either monorail just outside the hotel (the opening nearest the Transportation and Ticket Center). If you're on the resort monorail, you have to bend down to view Mickey through the lower part of the window (to the left of forward motion) and below the express monorail track next to you. On the express monorail, look to the right of forward motion.

Hint 200: Inside Chef Mickey's restaurant, a large side-profile Mickey decorates both sides of the large black, white, and red tile divider.

Hint 201: Ice cube trays on a shelf against the large central yellow pillar of Chef Mickey's buffet area have classic Mickey indentations.

Hint 202: Mickey ears are atop posts at the rear of Chef Mickey's restaurant.

Hint 203: On the lower part of the wall mural facing Contempo Café, the fourth girl from the right corner of the wall has a classic Mickey on her dress.

Hint 204: High on the wall mural facing Bay Lake, a black classic Mickey is on an owl perched on a girl's head. It's on the red right wing (as you face the mural).

Hint 205: On the fourth floor, a stick figure Mickey is in an artwork display on the side of the BVG Store facing the monorail.

Hint 206: On the fourth floor, classic Mickeys are in the carpet inside The Game Station Arcade.

Hint 207: Behind the main hotel, a classic Mickey silhouette can be found in the bricks under the metal Mickey Mouse sculpture. (The sculpture itself is a decorative Mickey, not a Hidden Mickey.)

Hint 208: In The Sand Bar by the pool, near the middle of the upper left wall border, one of the semaphore figures is wearing Mickey ears.

Hint 209: At the exit from the Garden Building to the parking lot (facing the monorail), a huge classic Mickey is traced in the tile under the exit canopy between the benches.

Hint 210: Large white classic Mickeys are frosted into glass partitions that support the curved roof that covers the vehicle drive-through entrance area to the hotel.

### -Bay Lake Tower

Hint 211: Classic Mickeys are at the top of both elevator towers at the sides of the hotel, and ceiling lights hang from Mickey-shaped metal plates. You can spot these from either the ground or the monorail.

## Shades of Green Resort

Hint 212: In the lobby, a Mickey statue stands in front of a framed picture of a blue sky with puffy clouds. Three classic Mickeys are in the clouds and another, made of fireworks, decorates the statue Mickey's right ear.

Hint 213: The Millpond pool is shaped as a classic Mickey. You can visit this pool outside or spot it on a resort map posted on hallway walls.

# Hither, Thither & Yon Scavenger Hunt

• • • • • • • • • • • • • • • • • • • • • • • • •

A car is the most efficient method for hunting the following areas. I've planned the hunt taking time of day and location into consideration. However, some backtracking will help keep you ahead of the crowds. Don't forget to be courteous to the shoppers, diners, golfers, swimmers, other guests, and Cast Members you encounter during your hunt. (Note: Because you may want to hunt only one area at a time, I've listed the perfect score for each area in parentheses after its name in the Clues section.)

As I advised in Chapter Six, pay attention to the Disney buses during your Hidden Mickey hunt around WDW property. You may get lucky! The Disney Cruise Line bus has a Hidden Pluto on each side of the gold scrollwork on the front of the bus between the headlights. One or more general Disney transport buses sometimes sports a classic Mickey on the rear of the bus, usually related to rear upper or lower lights. If you spot one or more of these images, give yourself 5 bonus points for each one.

## WDW Golf Courses (10 points)

If you're a golfer, look around for the following Hidden Mickeys:

Clue 1: Find a classic Mickey sand trap on the Magnolia Golf Course.
5 points

Clue 2: Look for a putting green shaped like Mickey Mouse at the Osprey Ridge Golf Course. You can visit this Hidden Mickey without playing golf. (Note: This area is being renovated, so this image may not be present.)
5 points

223

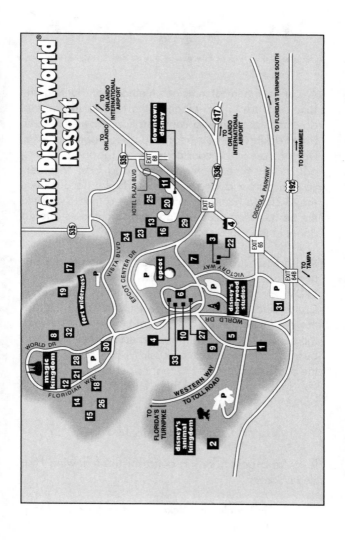

**1** All-Star Resorts
**2** Animal Kingdom Lodge
**3** Art of Animation (opening summer 2012)
**4** Beach Club
**5** Blizzard Beach
**6** BoardWalk
**7** Caribbean Beach
**8** Contemporary
**9** Coronado Springs
**10** Dolphin
**11** Downtown Disney
**12** Grand Floridian
**13** Lake Buena Vista Golf Course
**14** Magnolia Golf Course
**15** Oak Trail Golf Course
**16** Old Key West
**17** Osprey Ridge Golf Course

**18** Palm Golf Course
**19** Pioneer Hall
**20** Pleasure Island, in Downtown Disney
**21** Polynesian
**22** Pop Century
**23** Port Orleans – French Quarter
**24** Port Orleans – Riverside
**25** Saratoga Springs
**26** Shades of Green
**27** Swan
**28** Transportation and Ticket Center
**29** Typhoon Lagoon
**30** WDW Speedway
**31** ESPN Wide World of Sports Complex
**32** Wilderness Lodge
**33** Yacht Club
**P** Parking

225

## Vista Boulevard (5 points)

Clue 3: Drive east along Vista Boulevard away from Osprey Ridge Golf Course and stay alert for a classic Mickey on a sign to your left.
5 points

## WDW Speedway (5 points)

Clue 4: Go to the racetrack to take a look at the lake on the infield, or more accurately, a photo of it. The lake is barely visible from the fence around the parking area for the *Richard Petty Driving Experience*. So check out a framed photo of the racetrack inside the guest sign-in building to find this classic Mickey.
5 points

## WDW Water Parks (51 points)

★ *Blizzard Beach* (15 points)

Clue 5: Take a close look at the Beach Haus store's right rear wall near the dressing rooms.
3 points

Clue 6: Inside the Beach Haus, spot Hidden Mickeys near the merchandise.
2 points

Clue 7: Hop on the *Chairlift* to spot a classic Mickey formed by three round rocks on the ground near one of the support poles for the ride. (Tip: The Singles line for the *Chairlift* is usually shorter than the Standby line.)
5 points

Clue 8: Go to the rear of the park (by tube or on foot) to find a classic Mickey with a sorcerer's hat that's formed by three stones topped by a small triangular rock. (Psst! He's near the center of the side of a stone bridge that crosses over *Cross Country Creek*.)
5 points

★ *En Route to Typhoon Lagoon* (4 points)

Clue 9: On your way to Typhoon Lagoon from Blizzard Beach, spot Mickey on the Disney Vacation Club white tower, which

will appear on your left at the intersection of Buena
Vista Drive and Bonnet Creek Parkway.
4 points

★ *Typhoon Lagoon* (32 points)

Clue 10: Look around the *Crush 'n' Gusher* elevator
for a Hidden Mickey.
4 points

Clue 11: Search for Mickey on a bridge over *Castaway Creek*, near *Shark Reef*.
4 points

Clue 12: Marvel at Mickey if you snorkel with the
sharks in *Shark Reef*.
5 points

Clue 13: Find a classic Mickey near the entrance to the
steps to the *Storm Slides*.
3 points

Clue 14: Don't pass by Mickey on the steps up to the
*Storm Slides*.
4 points

Clue 15: Climb the trail up to *Humunga Kowabunga*
and locate a classic Mickey along the way.
4 points

Clue 16: Spot the Main Mouse hiding under a cannon
along *Castaway Creek* at the rear of the park.
4 points

Clue 17: Squint for Mickey in the wall of a cave at
*Ketchakiddee Creek*.
4 points

# ESPN Wide World of Sports
## (10 points)

Clue 18: Search hard for a three-dimensional Mickey
Mouse head near the high central ceiling of
The Milk House (the Field House). He's on
an upper rafter opposite the main entrance.
5 points

Clue 19: Don't miss Mickey in the outfield!
5 points

# Downtown Disney West Side
# (71 points)

## ★ *Cirque du Soleil* (8 points)

Clue 20: Look down for a Hidden Mickey in the sidewalk near Parking Lot Q.
5 points

Clue 21: Head for the outside restrooms (they're under the main entrance staircase to the theater) and examine the floor in either one (men's or women's). See a small classic Mickey?
3 points for either

## ★ *House of Blues* (3 points)

Clue 22: Search for a classic Mickey on the ceiling.
3 points

## ★ *DisneyQuest* (29 points)

Clue 23: Toward the end of the pre-show video, during the entrance elevator ride, find a classic Mickey formed by three small spheres. (Note: You may be directed to enter Ventureport directly, since the pre-show video is not always operational.)
3 points

Clue 24: Check the carpet on Ventureport's third floor.
3 points

Clue 25: Look for track lighting shaped like a classic Mickey on the second through fifth floors. (Psst! It's not on the same side on all four floors.)
5 points for spotting all four

Clue 26: Find similar lighting near "Invasion! An Extra-TERRORestrial Alien Encounter."
3 points

**228**

Clue 27: Spot classic Mickey markings on the back of one of the creatures you en-

counter during "Aladdin's Magic Carpet Ride." (You don't have to take the ride; you can watch the overhead video screens as others ride.)
4 points

★ Find two classic Hidden Mickeys at the "Virtual Jungle Cruise." (Again, you needn't take the ride; you can stand behind one of the ride pods and watch.)

Clue 28: Before the ride starts, watch the left side of the screen.
4 points

Clue 29: Keep watching the screen during the first part of the ride to see if the raft exits a glacier area. (The riders have optional routes, so they may not enter the glacier area.) If it does, watch carefully as it exits. (The ears on this Hidden Mickey aren't perfectly formed, but you'll recognize them.)
3 points

Clue 30: Along the queue for "Pirates of the Caribbean," examine the walls for Hidden Mickeys.
2 points

Clue 31: Check out both the trash can and the floor at the exit.
2 points for spotting Mickey on both

★ *Ridemakerz* (3 points)

Clue 32: Look around inside the store for Mickey images.
3 points for two or more

★ *Wolfgang Puck Café* (5 points)

Clue 33: Study the mosaic tile pyramid behind the reception counter to find a classic Hidden Mickey.
5 points

★ *Disney's Candy Cauldron* (4 points)

Clue 34: Go inside to find a classic Mickey marking on a stone.
4 points

**229**

★ *D Street* (17 points)

Clue 35: Spot Mickey on the ceiling.
2 points

Clue 36: Search for a small classic Mickey wall impression.
3 points

Clue 37: Observe Mickey in the bricks.
2 points

Clue 38: Find a Hidden Mickey on Mickey!
3 points

Clue 39: Look around for Mickey on a box.
4 points

Clue 40: Pluto is in the building!
3 points

★ *Pleasure Island Bus Stop* (2 points)

Clue 41: Look down near one of the bus stops.
2 points

# Downtown Disney Marketplace
# (156 points)

★ *Entrance to the Marketplace* (8 points)

Clue 42: Find Hidden Mickeys at the bus stop area near the main entrance.
5 points for five or more

Clue 43: Check out the signs over the entrances.
1 point for one or more

Clue 44: Study the green benches for Hidden Mickeys at the entrance and elsewhere around the Marketplace.
2 points

### ★ *Disney's Wonderful World of Memories* (3 points)

Clue 45: Search for Mickey outside the store.
3 points

### ★ *Disney's Days of Christmas* (11 points)

Clue 46: Step inside and search for a Mickey made of rocks.
3 points

Clue 47: Find at least one classic Mickey on each of three large trees.
4 points total for one or more on each tree

Clue 48: Take a good look at the ceiling in the rear room of the shop.
2 points

Clue 49: Check out the walls in the rear room.
2 points

### ★ *Goofy's Candy Company* (10 points)

Clue 50: Search for a Goofy shadow in the store.
4 points

Clue 51: Find Goofy and other characters on the wall.
4 points for three or more characters

Clue 52: Find Mickey in a store window.
2 points

### ★ *Cap'n Jack's Restaurant* (3 points)

Clue 53: Step inside the restaurant entrance and spot Mickey.
3 points

### ★ *Sassagoula River Cruise ferry* (5 points)

Clue 54: If you have time, take the *Sassagoula River Cruise* ferryboat to Port Orleans – French Quarter, then disembark and ride the next boat back to the Downtown Disney Marketplace. During both your crossings, study

the Treehouse Villas for Hidden Mickeys.
5 points for one or more

### ★ *Marketplace Carrousel* (5 points)

Clue 55: Study the decorative panels on the Carrousel for four classic Mickeys.
5 points for spotting all four

### ★ *Mickey's Pantry* (3 points)

Clue 56: Spot classic Mickeys on the walls.
3 points for three or more

### ★ *Once Upon A Toy* (31 points)

(Note: This store sports numerous Mickeys and other Disney characters in the décor in addition to the Hidden Mickeys below.)

Clue 57: Examine the interactive fountain near the store. (Note: Two Hidden Mickeys are there all the time, a third appears only when the water is on.)
4 points for two; 5 points for spotting all three

Clue 58: Find classic Mickeys in the cement outside.
2 points

Clue 59: Outside the main entrance, look for classic Mickeys with tires for ears.
2 points

★ Now enter the store and keep your eyes open.

Clue 60: Gaze up for classic Mickeys.
2 points

Clue 61: Check out the tops of merchandise stands. (Only some sport Hidden Mickeys.)
1 point for one or more

Clue 62: Now examine the bottoms of these stands.
1 point for one or more

Clue 63: Search for a classic Mickey on a sandal in the middle of the first room.
3 points

Clue 64: Examine the mural behind the service desk in the same room.
2 points for two or more images

Clue 65: Look at the upper beams of the wooden merchandise displays.
1 point for one or more

Clue 66: Now observe the bolts on those displays.
1 point

Clue 67: Study the floor for a Mickey.
3 points

Clue 68: Find a classic Hidden Mickey cloud in a central room.
3 points

Clue 69: Look for a Mickey shadow in a central room.
3 points

Clue 70: Look for Hidden Mickey lollipops.
2 points

★ *Disney's Pin Traders* (3 points)

Clue 71: Spot a Mickey on a statue inside the store.
3 points

★ *Tren-D* (9 points)

Clue 72: Look around for Mickey on a merchandise table.
3 points

Clue 73: Check out Mickey on the walls.
2 points

Clue 74: Find Mickey on a mannequin.
4 points

★ *Team Mickey Athletic Club* (5 points)

Clue 75: Find a classic Mickey in the Disney Vacation Club (DVC) display near Team Mickey.
2 points

233

Clue 76: Observe the pillars outside.
1 point

Clue 77: Inside the store, check the tops of the mannequin heads and merchandise stands.
2 points for two types

### ★ *Ghirardelli Ice Cream and Chocolate Shop* (4 points)

Clue 78: Locate Mickey on a wall inside.
4 points

### ★ *Near the lake* (3 points)

Clue 79: Do you see any chairs with Hidden Mickeys outside the Ghirardelli Shop?
2 points

Clue 80: Spot Mickeys in the fence around the lake.
1 point

### ★ *World of Disney* (48 points)

Clue 81: Look up for Mickeys on the store sign.
1 point

Clue 82: Find light brown Mickeys outside the store.
2 points

Clue 83: Look for classic Mickeys in some of the clothing racks.
2 points

Clue 84: Examine some of the indoor signs for an image of Mickey.
2 points

Clue 85: Find a classic Mickey emblem on the Chinese Theater in a wall mural in the high-ceilinged central room.
4 points

Clue 86: In the same room, find an upside-down classic Mickey on the Pocahontas airship.
4 points

★ Now find two classic Mickeys on the Tweedle Dee and Tweedle Dum mural in the same room.

Clue 87: Look for a flag.
2 points

Clue 88: Check out an apron.
2 points

Clue 89: Study the mannequins.
4 points

Clue 90: Find Mickey near Cinderella Castle.
4 points

Clue 91: Search for two different classic Mickeys inside shadowboxes on the wall.
3 points for both

Clue 92: Spot classic Mickeys on paintings in the central Genie Room.
2 points

Clue 93: In the same room, observe the "antique" maps decorating the walls. (Psst! Think character profiles.)
5 points for three or more

Clue 94: Next door in the Villain Room, spot Cruella DeVille's Hidden Mickey.
3 points

Clue 95: Look down for Mickey under merchandise.
3 points

Clue 96: Now find Mickey on a wall near the Princess Room.
2 points

Clue 97: Outside the store, in an entrance area to the Marketplace, look around for a classic Mickey.
3 points

★ *T-Rex Café* (5 points)

Clue 98: Admire a classic Mickey near the bar area.
5 points

## WDW Casting Center (3 points)

Clue 99: Drive to the Casting building, across the road from the rightmost Downtown Disney Marketplace entrance, to locate more classic Mickeys. (These Hidden Mickeys can also be spotted from Interstate 4.)
3 points

## Miniature Golf Courses (20 points)

You can find these Hidden Mickeys while you play the courses. Or you may be able to walk the courses without playing if it's not crowded, due to rain or luck. (Tell the attendants that you're hunting Hidden Mickeys and ask if you can take a look around.)

### ★ *Fantasia Gardens* (4 points)

Clue 100: Check the tee-off areas.
1 point

Clue 101: Take a good look at the 12th hole on the Gardens Course.
3 points

### ★ *Winter Summerland* (16 points)

Clue 102: Find Mickey on the third hole.
3 points

★ Now head straight for the 16th holes.

Clue 103: Spot Goofy and Donald on the 16th hole of the Winter Course.
3 points

Clue 104: Now check around the same hole for a Mickey Mouse gingerbread cookie.
2 points

Clue 105: Don't miss the Mickey ornament in the same area!
2 points

 Clue 106: Find Mickey and Minnie on the 16th hole of the Summer Course. (Psst! This

Hidden Mickey is also visible from the 16th and 17th holes of the Winter Course.)
3 points

Clue 107: Study the Christmas tree on the 17th hole of the Summer Course for Hidden Mickeys.
3 points for three Hidden Mickeys

## Near Celebration, Florida (4 points)

Okay, I admit it; this Mickey isn't hidden. Just the opposite, in fact. But it is unique. So I decided to include it anyway. You'll find a huge classic Mickey near Celebration, Florida, on the west side of Interstate 4.

Clue 108: Look for it as you get close to Exit 62.
4 points

## Near the Magic Kingdom (5 points)

Clue 109: You can only see this classic Mickey made of tree groves from the air or on an image from a Google search. It's a few miles northwest of the Magic Kingdom. Good luck!
5 points

### Total Points for Hither, Thither & Yon =

### How'd you do?

A perfect score for this hunt is 340, and you may have done even better if you earned bonus points on the Disney buses. You'll find a breakdown by area on the following page, so that you can tally your score for only those places you've covered.

Give yourself Gold if you scored at least 80% of available points, Bronze if you scored at least 40%.

**The Golf Courses (10)**
    Magnolia Golf Course (5)
    Osprey Ridge Golf Club (5)
**Vista Blvd. (5)**
**WDW Speedway (5)**
**WDW Water Parks (51)**
    Blizzard Beach (15)
    En route to Typhoon Lagoon (4)
    Typhoon Lagoon (32)
**ESPN Wide World of Sports (10)**
**Downtown Disney West Side (71)**
    Cirque du Soleil (8)
    House of Blues (3)
    DisneyQuest (29)
    Ridemakerz (3)
    Wolfgang Puck Café (5)
    Disney's Candy Cauldron (4)
    D-Street (17)
    Pleasure Island Bus Stop (2)
**Downtown Disney Marketplace (156)**
    Entrance to the Marketplace (8)
    Disney's Wonderful World of Memories store (3)
    Disney's Days of Christmas (11)
    Goofy's Candy Co. (10)
    Cap'n Jack's Restaurant (3)
    Sassagoula River Cruise Ferry (5)
    Marketplace Carrousel (5)
    Mickey's Pantry (3)
    Once Upon A Toy (31)
    Disney's Pin Traders (3)
    Tren-D (9)
    Team Mickey Athletic Club (5)
    Ghirardelli Ice Cream and Chocolate Shop (4)
    Near the lake (3)
    World of Disney (48)
    T-Rex Café (5)
**WDW Casting Center (3)**
**Miniature Golf Courses (20)**
    Fantasia Gardens (4)
    Winter Summerland (16)
**Near Celebration, Florida (4)**
**Near the Magic Kingdom (5)**

**Caution:
Don't peek at this
section unless you
really want help!**

## The Golf Courses

### -Magnolia Golf Course

Hint 1: A sand trap at the sixth green is shaped like a classic Mickey.

### -Osprey Ridge Golf Club

Hint 2: The practice putting green is shaped like a side profile of Mickey Mouse.

## Vista Boulevard

Hint 3: If you drive east from Osprey Ridge Golf Course along Vista Boulevard, you can spot a sign for the Golden Oak Resort on your left. A classic Mickey is hidden in the tree of Golden Oak's logo.

## WDW Speedway

Hint 4: A lake on the infield is shaped like a classic Mickey. You'll barely see the

lake, let alone the Hidden Mickey, from ground level. To marvel at its full effect without paying admission, walk inside the guest sign-in building and look at the framed photo on the wall.

# Water Parks

### -Blizzard Beach

Hint 5: Find a lighting fixture on the wall at the right rear of the Beach Haus store near the dressing rooms. There's a painting on the cover in which a small classic Mickey is formed by rocks at the lower center of an outdoor mountain scene.

Hint 6: As in many WDW shops, one or more of the merchandise stands has classic Mickey-shaped holes on its center pole.

Hint 7: From the *Chairlift* ride that takes you to the water slides, look to the ground on the second level of the mountain just past support pole #4 (counting from the beginning of the lift) to spot a classic Mickey made of three round rocks.

Hint 8: At the rear of the park, a classic Mickey is formed by three stones jutting out from near the top edge of a stone bridge crossing *Cross Country Creek*. It is on the side of the bridge, near the center. A small triangular rock over this Hidden Mickey gives it the appearance of wearing a sorcerer's hat.

(Tip: You can see this Mickey from the water or dry land. It is visible from the floating tubes as you approach the bridge and, on land, you can see it through the trees either from in front of the *Runoff Rapids* entrance sign or from several points on the walkway on the other side of the bridge.)

### -En Route to Typhoon Lagoon

Hint 9: Classic Mickey holes are in the railing around the Disney Vacation Club (DVC) white tower that stands to the left of Buena Vista Drive at its intersection with Bonnet Creek Parkway.

### -Typhoon Lagoon

Hint 10: At *Crush 'n' Gusher,* on the upper floor near the elevator, paint circles on the cement form a classic Mickey.

Hint 11: Mickey ears are at the bottom of a vertical strut in the railing of a bridge. You can see the ears if you enter *Castaway Creek* at Shark Landing (near *Shark Reef*) and look behind you as you float under the first bridge. The ears are toward the right side of the bridge. You can also usually see the ears if you walk downstream on either side of the creek and look back at the bridge.

Hint 12: As you snorkel along in *Shark Reef,* you can often see a classic Mickey resting on the bottom of the swim route. Recently, the Mickey was located on the right side, about halfway along the route after the island.

Hint 13: Before you reach the entrance to the walkway to the *Storm Slides,* and to the left of the outside shower, three short logs in the ground form an upside-down classic Mickey when viewed from above.

Hint 14: About halfway up the wooden steps to the *Storm Slides,* Mickey ears are on the left side of a walkway slat, just before the large anchor on the right side of the path.

Hint 15: Near the end of the long trail up to *Humunga Kowabunga,* three of the last short logs in the ground under the rope fence to the left of the walkway form an upside-down classic Mickey when viewed from above.

Hint 16: You'll find a classic Mickey formed by cannonballs along *Castaway Creek.* He's on your left by the second cannon past the waterfall if you're drifting in the creek. If you're walking on the nearby trail, you'll see him just past Forgotten Grotto in the rear of the park as you walk alongside the drifters.

Hint 17: In the walk-through cave at the rear of *Ketchakiddee Creek,* a classic Mickey hole is in the rock. It's on the back wall of the cave, about one and a half feet up from the ground, and near the drain at the right side of the cave as you enter the cave from the water.

## ESPN Wide World of Sports

Hint 18: A three-dimensional Mickey Mouse head looks out over the court from near the high central ceiling in The Milk House (the Field House). He's on an upper rafter above the sign, "The Milk House," in front of a yellow triangular wall partition that is opposite the main entrance. I spotted him to the upper left of the lower seats of section 104.

Hint 19: A large, pale green classic Mickey image lies in the outfield grass in the Wide World of Sports baseball stadium.

## Downtown Disney West Side

### -Cirque du Soleil

Hint 20: A classic Mickey is etched in the sidewalk near *Cirque du Soleil,* on the second slab back from Parking Lot Q, just past a manhole cover and near the grass.

Hint 21: Under the main entrance staircase to the show are restrooms for men and women. You will find tiles laid to approximate a small classic Hidden Mickey on the floor of each restroom, in a corner just inside the entrance doors. These circles don't touch, but the design is convincing enough for my eyes.

### -House of Blues

Hint 22: Walk through the front door and down the right side aisle. A classic Mickey is on the ceiling past the first server's station.

### -DisneyQuest

Hint 23: Toward the end of the pre-show video, during the entrance elevator ride, a classic Mickey is formed by three spheres

at the bottom of a ray gun. For me, this Hidden Mickey is more convincing than the spheres at the bottom of the large three-dimensional ray gun poised over the lobby of Ventureport. (Note: The pre-show video is not always operational.)

Hint 24: Symbols and figures that include classic Mickey designs are woven into the carpet on the third floor in Ventureport.

Hint 25: Track lighting shaped like a classic Mickey hangs above the elevator doors on floors two, three, four, and five. You'll find it near the "Mighty Ducks Pinball Slam" (on the third floor) and near "Ride the Comix" (on the fourth and fifth floors). On the second floor, near "CyberSpace Mountain," the lighting is above an elevator door on the opposite side of the elevator bank.

Hint 26: Similar track lighting can be found in front of pod 4 of "Invasion! An ExtraTERRORestrial Alien Encounter."

Hint 27: During "Aladdin's Magic Carpet Ride," the golden beetle you encounter bears classic Mickey markings on its back.

Hint 28: At the "Virtual Jungle Cruise," classic Mickey-shaped balloons periodically float up from the left side of the screen, in front of the castle, before the ride starts.

Hint 29: On the screen in the first part of the "Virtual Jungle Cruise" ride, the raft may exit a glacier area under a distorted classic Mickey-shaped ice bridge over the river.

Hint 30: In the wall murals along the queue for "Pirates of the Caribbean," the rightmost set of palm tree coconuts near the stairs is shaped like a classic Mickey.

Hint 31: You can spot the DisneyQuest classic Mickey logo on trash cans (like the one near the exit). It is also illuminated on the floor of the exit walkway and, at times, on the walkways outside DisneyQuest.

### -Ridemakerz

Hint 32: Small classic Mickey stickers and impressions are placed in random locations on the walls and pillars inside the store.

### -Wolfgang Puck Café

Hint 33: Behind the reception counter, about two thirds of the way up the mosaic pyramid, a white tile and two smaller black tiles form a classic Mickey. Search for it to the right of a tall ceramic vessel standing on a shelf.

### -Disney's Candy Cauldron

Hint 34: Inside the store, on the upper wall above the candy display, a dark marking on a stone near the ceiling forms a classic Hidden Mickey.

### -D Street

Hint 35: Above you, on the ceiling just inside the store entrance, various Mickey images float as clouds.

Hint 36: A somewhat distorted image on the wall to your immediate left as you enter the store resembles a classic Mickey.

Hint 37: A large classic Mickey image is formed by exposed bricks on the wall behind the main counter and across from the store entrance.

Hint 38: On the wall to the right of the exposed-brick classic Mickey, a full-body menacing Mickey has a black classic Mickey on his belt buckle.

Hint 39: A classic Mickey made of black smudges is on the back of a display box near the front entrance inside the store.

Hint 40: A Hidden Pluto made of exposed bricks is on the right front wall of the store.

### -Pleasure Island Bus Stop

Hint 41: A large classic Mickey hides in the cement between Bus Stops 5 and 6, across from Planet Hollywood restaurant.

## Downtown Disney Marketplace

### -Entrance to the Marketplace

Hint 42: Coca-Cola vending machines stand near Bus Stops 2, 3, and 4 in the Downtown Disney Marketplace Bus Stop area. In colorful paintings on these machines, one full-body Mickey is pouring water and several classic Mickeys can be found on signs, a tower, and an awning.

Hint 43: Signs over the entrances to the Marketplace sport classic Mickeys at their sides.

Hint 44: Green benches with classic Mickey emblems on the top and sides are scattered around the Marketplace and the interactive fountain.

### -Disney's Wonderful World of Memories

Hint 45: The sign on the store contains a full-figure Hidden Mickey on the page of a book.

### -Disney's Days of Christmas

Hint 46: A large dark brown circular rock and two smaller rocks for "ears" form a classic Mickey on the middle side of the "chimney" in the store. You'll see Dalmatians on the mantelpiece around this chimney.

Hint 47: Inside the shop, three large trees surrounded by merchandise have classic Mickeys carved in their bark near the tops of their trunks. The trees are not Christmas trees, and each of the three has one or two Mickey carvings.

Hint 48: In the rear room of the shop, classic Mickeys hide in the scrollwork on the ceiling.

Hint 49: Also in the rear room, you'll find small white classic Mickeys in the wallpaper near the ceiling.

### -Goofy's Candy Co.

Hint 50: A shadow of Goofy is on the upper back wall of the store, behind the large Krispy Treat display.

Hint 51: Goofy, Mickey Mouse, Pluto, and other characters hide in the light brown mural on the upper wall around the store.

Hint 52: Classic Mickey circles are part of the design in the middle of the side window that faces the lagoon.

### -Cap'n Jack's Restaurant

Hint 53: Three glass or plastic balls in a net form a classic Mickey behind the check-in counter that's just inside the restaurant entrance.

### -Sassagoula River Cruise ferry

Hint 54: From the boat dock to the right of Cap'n Jack's Restaurant, take the ferryboat to Port Orleans – French Quarter and then back to Downtown Disney Marketplace. Both ways, spot small white classic Mickeys in some of the Treehouse Villas' windows.

### -Marketplace Carrousel

Hint 55: At least four classic Mickeys are hiding on the inner and outer decorative panels on the Carrousel near Disney's Days of Christmas store. Look for (1) a blue classic Mickey on the sign under Minnie Mouse; (2) two light green classic Mickeys on the dragon's nose; (3) two tiny classic Mickeys on the pink window awnings on the right side of the panel that shows part of the store from a distance, and (4) pink classic Mickeys formed of roses in the upper part of the panels in the center of the Carrousel.

### -Mickey's Pantry

Hint 56: You'll find classic Mickeys of different sizes and colors in the wall decorations around the store.

### -Once Upon A Toy

Hint 57: In the interactive flat fountain near the Once Upon A Toy store, water-tube heads are shaped like classic Mickeys, recessed lights in the cement are arranged in a classic Mickey shape, and the fountain water collects into a huge classic Mickey on the cement!

Hint 58: Outside the store, you'll find several classic Mickeys in the cement near the side entrance.

Hint 59: Outside the store's main entrance, classic Mickeys are formed by truck tires (the ears) atop Lincoln Logs.

Hint 60: Classic Mickey pincers or clamps (holding toys) circulate on a track that hangs from the ceiling in the room with Mr. Potato Head.

Hint 61: Tinker Toys on top of merchandise stands around the store form classic Mickeys.

Hint 62: At the bottom of these merchandise stands, you'll find classic Mickey supports.

Hint 63: Two black classic Mickeys are on blue sandals on one of the Mr. Potato Heads in the first room just inside the store's main entrance.

Hint 64: In this same room, the mural behind a service desk includes a classic Mickey balloon, several pairs of Mickey ears, and a Mickey ice cream bar.

Hint 65: The centers of the upper beams on wooden merchandise displays sport classic Mickey shapes.

Hint 66: Also on the wooden merchandise displays, large wing nuts on some of the bolts form Mickey ears.

Hint 67: Across the first and second rooms (as you enter from the front main entrance), large letters in Scrabble tiles on the floor spell "MICKEY."

Hint 68: In a central room of the store, a classic Mickey cloud appears in a window in a mural behind the service desk.

Hint 69: In the same room, a partial classic Mickey shadow is at the top of a wall mural. It's to the left of the classic Mickey cloud and above a checkout counter.

Hint 70: In the rear room, lollipops are arranged to form classic Mickeys on the outside of merchandise stands.

### -Disney's Pin Traders

Hint 71: On the large statue of Mickey and Minnie, Mickey wears a classic Mickey pin on his tie.

### -Tren-D

Hint 72: A classic Mickey is on the top of a merchandise table just inside the Tren-D entrance doors from the main promenade.

Hint 73: Classic Mickeys are repeated in sections of framed wallpaper artwork inside the store.

Hint 74: A tiny black classic Mickey is on a female mannequin's cheek, under the left eye.

### -Team Mickey Athletic Club

Hint 75: Outside the entrance to Team Mickey, you'll find a classic Mickey repeated in the white picket fence bordering the Disney Vacation Club display.

Hint 76: Classic Mickeys are on the bases and tops of the shop's outside pillars.

Hint 77: Some of the mannequin heads and merchandise stands inside the store are topped with classic Mickeys, with a basketball for the head and a baseball and a tennis ball for the ears.

### -Ghirardelli Ice Cream and Chocolate Shop

Hint 78: A dark side-profile image of Mickey looking to the left appears as a shadow in a painting on a rear wall of the shop (to the left as you enter). Look for a streetcar in the painting. The shadow is in the streetcar's second window from the left.

### -Near the lake

Hint 79: Green chairs with classic Mickeys on top are scattered around outside in the Marketplace and near the Ghirardelli shop.

Hint 80: Several sections of the green fence around the lake have repeating classic Mickeys near the top of the railing.

### -World of Disney

Hint 81: Blue classic Mickeys are at the ends of the World of Disney entrance signs.

Hint 82: Light brown classic Mickeys can be found near the tops of the columns outside the store.

Hint 83: Classic Mickey holes are drilled in some of the metal posts that hold up clothing racks.

Hint 84: Some of the indoor signs for the various store sections include Mickey and other character images.

Hint 85: In the high-ceilinged central room, behind the three little pigs floating overhead, a wall mural has a classic Mickey emblem above the doors of the Chinese Theater.

Hint 86: In the same room, the Pocahontas airship has an upside-down classic Mickey at the very bottom of the rear vertical tail fin, near where the tail fin connects to the body of the airship.

Hint 87: In the same room, you'll find a classic Mickey on a flag in the background of the Tweedle Dee and Tweedle Dum wall mural.

Hint 88: That mural also includes a classic Mickey on Tweedle Dee's apron.

Hint 89: In the same room of the store, some of the female mannequins have classic Mickey freckles under their eyes.

Hint 90: In the large central room, the clouds that encircle the model of Cinderella Castle hide a small classic Mickey.

Hint 91: In the large central room, you'll find several wood-framed shadowboxes decorating the walls. Each contains a framed full-body white silhouette of Mickey Mouse (a décor Mickey) positioned against a red background in a fancy black diamond-shaped frame. A small red classic Mickey hides in the black frame's bottom tip. In the background, white classic Mickeys form the centers of black stylized flowers in the black and white paper that lines the shadowbox and forms the background for the black frame and its contents.

Hint 92: On the walls in the central Genie Room, blue classic Mickeys can be spotted in the compass paintings.

Hint 93: Also on the Genie Room walls, antique-looking maps on wood panels painted to look like tapestries have land masses that resemble the side profiles of Mickey Mouse, Winnie the Pooh, Goofy, and possibly Donald Duck. (Donald is a bit of a stretch.)

Hint 94: On the wall in the Villain Room, next door to the Genie Room, Cruella DeVille's left wrist is wrapped with fur that has a classic Mickey dark spot on the side.

Hint 95: Classic Mickey "feet" are at the bottom of display tubs that hold merchandise in some of the rooms (and decorative classic Mickeys may surround the top edges of these tubs).

Hint 96: At the far end of the store, on the walls along the short hallway to the restrooms from the Princess Room, two picture frames are lined with small classic Mickeys.

Hint 97: Near the World of Disney store, in an entrance to Downtown Disney from the parking lot, three pots form a classic Mickey fountain.

### -T-Rex Café

Hint 98: Just inside the entrance and over the bar, a pink classic Mickey hides on the body of an octopus across from a green praying mantis.

## WDW Casting Center

Hint 99: Classic Mickey holes can be seen in the upper outside walls of the Casting building. (These Hidden Mickeys can also be spotted from Interstate 4.)

## WDW Miniature Golf Courses

### -Fantasia Gardens

Hint 100: The tee-off areas on both courses are marked with classic Mickeys.

Hint 101: On the Gardens Course, the green at the 12th hole is shaped like a classic Mickey.

### -Winter Summerland

Hint 102: On the third hole of the Winter Course, candy canes, milk, and gingerbread men pop out of "Defrosty the cooler." One is a gingerbread cookie featuring Mickey ears.

Hint 103: On the 16th hole of the Winter Course, you'll find Goofy and Donald nutcrackers on the left side of the mantelpiece.

Hint 104: A Mickey Mouse gingerbread cookie pokes out from a stocking hanging on the right side of the same mantelpiece.

Hint 105: A gold classic Mickey ornament is hanging on the left side.

Hint 106: On the left side of the 16th hole of the Summer Course, Mickey and Minnie Mouse are sitting in a sleigh on the mantelpiece, along with Pluto. Since the 16th holes of both courses are close together, this mantelpiece is also visible from the 16th and 17th holes of the Winter Course.

Hint 107: At least three classic Mickey ornaments hang on the Christmas tree at the 17th hole of the Summer Course.

## Near Celebration, Florida

Hint 108: On the west side of Interstate 4, south of exit 62 near Celebration, you'll find a huge classic Mickey atop an electrical transmission line pole.

## Near the Magic Kingdom

Hint 109: A few miles northwest of the Magic Kingdom, a huge green classic Mickey made of groves of trees can only be seen from the air (or on a Google image). The Hidden Mickey is in a field just off Highway 27 and near the 192 merge.

# Other Mickey Appearances

• • • • • • • • • • • • • • • • • • • • • • • •

These Hidden Mickeys won't earn you any points, but you're bound to enjoy them if you're in the right place at the right time to see them.

★ Look for holiday Hidden Mickeys if you're at WDW during the Christmas season or any major holiday. For example, the "Osborne Family Spectacle of Dancing Lights" along the backlot area at Disney's Hollywood Studios includes many hiding Mickeys.

★ Other "Hidden" Mickeys — décor and deliberate — appear with some regularity throughout WDW. Notice the Mickster on WDW brochures, maps and flags, Cast Member nametags, guestroom keys, pay telephones and phone books, and restaurant and store receipts. The restaurants sometimes offer classic Mickey butter and margarine pats, pancakes and waffles, pizzas and pasta, as well as Mickeys on napkins and food trays. They also arrange dishes and condiments to form classic Mickeys, and some condiment containers are shaped like Mickey.

The Mickey hat and ears on top of the "Earful Tower" are obvious to every visitor in the vicinity of Disney's Hollywood Studios. Many road signs on WDW Resort property sport Mickey ears and classic Mickey images, and WDW vehicles and monorails have Mickey Mouse images and insignia.

Cleaning personnel will often spray the ground, windows, furniture, and other items with three circles of cleaning solution (a classic Mickey) before the final cleansing. Or they may leave three wet Mickey Mouse circles or other Disney character images on the pavement after mopping! Mickey even decorates manhole covers, survey markers, and utility covers in the ground, as you've had a chance to find out for yourself on some of the scavenger hunts.

Enjoy all these Mickeys as you explore WDW. And if you want to take some home with you, rest assured that you can always find "Hidden" Mickeys on souvenir mugs, merchandise bags and boxes, T-shirts, and Christmas tree ornaments sold in the Disney World shops. So even when you're far away from WDW, you can continue to enjoy Hidden Mickeys.

# My Favorite Hidden Mickeys

•  •  •  •  •  •  •  •  •  •  •  •  •  •  •  •  •  •  •  •  •  •

In this book, I've described over 1,000 Hidden Mickeys at Walt Disney World. I enjoy every one of them, but the following are extra special to me. They're special because of their uniqueness, their deep camouflage (which makes them especially hard to find), or the "Eureka!" response they elicit when I spot them—or any combination of the above. Here then are my Top Ten Hidden Mickeys and, not far behind, Ten Honorable Mentions. I apologize to you if your favorite Hidden Mickey is not (yet) on the lists below.

## My Top Ten

**1.** Mickey hiding behind the fern on the big mural inside the Garden Grill restaurant, The Land pavilion, Epcot. When I outline this Mickey (a Cast Member often helps me by handing me a broom to reach it and highlighting it with a flashlight), I have witnessed folks in the restaurant smile and shout, "I see him; look, there's Mickey!" (Chap. 3, Clue 104)

**2.** The "Grim Reaper" Mickey, *The Haunted Mansion*, Liberty Square, Magic Kingdom. A classic, this wonderful Mickey image has survived refurbishments and seems even better and spookier than ever! (Chap. 2, Clue 34)

**3.** Minnie Mouse's shadow on the mural by the loading dock, *The Great Movie Ride*, Disney's Hollywood Studios. Hard to spot but once you see her, you'll never forget her. (Chap. 4, Clue 33)

**4.** Mickey peeking out of a hole in an overhead beam in the lobby of the Wilderness Lodge Villas. Outstanding effect! Most folks don't even know he's up there, hiding! (Chap. 6, Clue 161)

**5.** The golf ball Mickey, *Soarin'*, The Land, Epcot. Your first reaction is to duck down to

**255**

avoid the ball that's flying right at you. But stay still and don't blink, or you'll miss this great Hidden Mickey! (Chap. 3, Clue 6)

**6.** Mickey in rocks, Japan, World Showcase, Epcot. This is one amazingly well-concealed rock Mickey! (Chap. 3, Clue 74)

**7.** The classic Mickey on a globe in the Yacht Club Resort lobby. People come from afar to admire this tiny blue Mickey image, and the friendly Cast Members are more than happy to help you find it. (Chap. 6, Clue 122)

**8.** Mickey sitting on the edge of the roof of a backstage building next to the Contemporary Resort. This playful Mickey welcomes you to the Magic Kingdom. When you're on the monorail, show this Mickey to fellow travelers; they'll be amazed! (Chap. 6, Clue 199)

**9.** Mickey along the *Star Tours: The Adventures Continue* entrance queue, Disney's Hollywood Studios. He's on a tree trunk, directly across from the Imperial Walker. High above the walkway and hard to spot, The Force is definitely with this Mickey! (Chap. 4, Clue 44)

**10.** Mickey sitting with Donald on the wall, "Raiders of the Lost Ark" scene, *The Great Movie Ride*, Disney's Hollywood Studios. A real regal Mickey. (Chap. 4, Clue 39)

## Ten Honorable Mentions

**1.** A classic Mickey traced in the cement near *Astro Orbiter*, Tomorrowland, the Magic Kingdom. This image has faded over time, but it's still worth the effort to locate it. (Chap. 2, Clue 61)

**2.** The utility cover classic Mickey by the Tamu Tamu Refreshment Shop, Africa, Disney's Animal Kingdom. The mundane utility cover transformed. (Chap. 5, Clue 93)

**3).** Sorcerer Mickey at the rear of Blizzard Beach formed by stones jutting out from a bridge over *Cross Country Creek*. Very clever! (Chap. 7, Clue 8)

**4.** Mickey in the vines outside the rear lobby doors, Animal Kingdom Lodge Resort. Well camouflaged and hard to find, but fun to spot. (Chap. 6, Clue 7)

**5.** A classic Mickey in tile on the counter at the Kona Island coffee bar, Polynesian Resort. This one's a real winner, especially when you point it out to folks who've never seen it. It's hiding in plain sight! (Chap. 6, Clue 175)

**6.** Two large, faint classic Mickeys on red brick out-door walls at Saratoga Springs Resort. One's in the Springs section (across from the check-in parking lot), the other's in Congress Park (near the lagoon). Amazingly creative brickwork! (Chap. 6, Clues 90 & 91)

**7.** A small classic Mickey etched in the cement outside the Old Port Royale pool, Caribbean Beach Resort, on a sidewalk to the main parking lot. One of the best examples of a Mickey image in cement, it's rewarding to track down this Mickey! (Chap. 6, Clue 66)

**8.** The classic Mickey made of three round rocks on the ground under the *Chairlift* ride, Blizzard Beach. Stay alert as you ride to the water slides; this Mickey is only visible as you pass over it in your lift! (Chap. 7, Clue 7)

**9.** The classic Mickey embedded in the stonework of the fireplace in the Carolwood Pacific Railroad Room in Wilderness Lodge Villas. He's one of many inventive Hidden Mickeys at the Wilderness Lodge Resort. (Chap. 6, Clue 164)

**10.** The small "Mortimer & Co, 1928, Contractors" impressions in the cement sidewalks of Sunset Boulevard in Disney's Hollywood Studios. Mortimer Mouse was Mickey Mouse's first (and soon discarded) name; 1928 was the year he was "born." A nice tribute to Mickey! (Chap. 4, Clue 119)

# CHAPTER 10

# Don't Stop Now!

Hidden Mickey mania is contagious. The benign pastime of searching out Hidden Mickeys has escalated into a bona fide vacation mission for many Walt Disney World fans. I'm proud to include myself among them. Searching for images of the Main Mouse can enhance a solo trip to the parks or a vacation for the entire family. Little ones delight in spotting and greeting Mickey Mouse characters in the parks and restaurants. As children grow, the Hidden Mickey game is a natural evolution of their fondness for the Mouse.

Join the search! With alert eyes and mind, you can spot Hidden Mickey classics and new Hidden Mickeys just waiting to be found. Even beginners have happened upon a new, unreported Hidden Mickey or two. As new attractions open and older ones get refurbished, new Hidden Mickeys await discovery.

It may be just my imagination but I swear that every time I visit Walt Disney World, I spot a Hidden Mickey up in the clouds, watching over his domain! Do you think the Imagineers might actually have some influence on the atmosphere over Walt Disney World?

The Disney entertainment phenomenon is unique in many ways, and Hidden Mickey mania is one manifestation of Disney's universal appeal. Join in the fun! Maybe I'll see you at Walt Disney World, marveling (like me) at these Hidden Gems. They're waiting patiently for you to discover them.

Note: This Index includes only those rides, restaurants, hotels, and other places and attractions that harbor confirmed Hidden Mickeys. So if the attraction you're looking for isn't included, Mickey isn't hiding there. Or if he is, I haven't yet spotted him. – *Steve Barrett*

The following abbreviations appear in this Index:

| | | |
|---|---|---|
| AK | - | Disney's Animal Kingdom |
| DD | - | Downtown Disney |
| DH | - | Disney's Hollywood Studios |
| E | - | Epcot |
| MK | - | Magic Kingdom |
| R | - | Located in a Resort hotel complex |
| WP | - | Water Park |

## M